"*Dinosaurs* is an engaging and inviting book, full of factual information that goes far beyond what the title promises. This book isn't just about dinosaurs; it's about the entire history of life, and it is beautiful."

——————

STEVE BRUSATTE
University of Edinburgh paleontologist and *New York Times* bestselling author of *The Rise and Fall of the Dinosaurs*

DINOSAURS

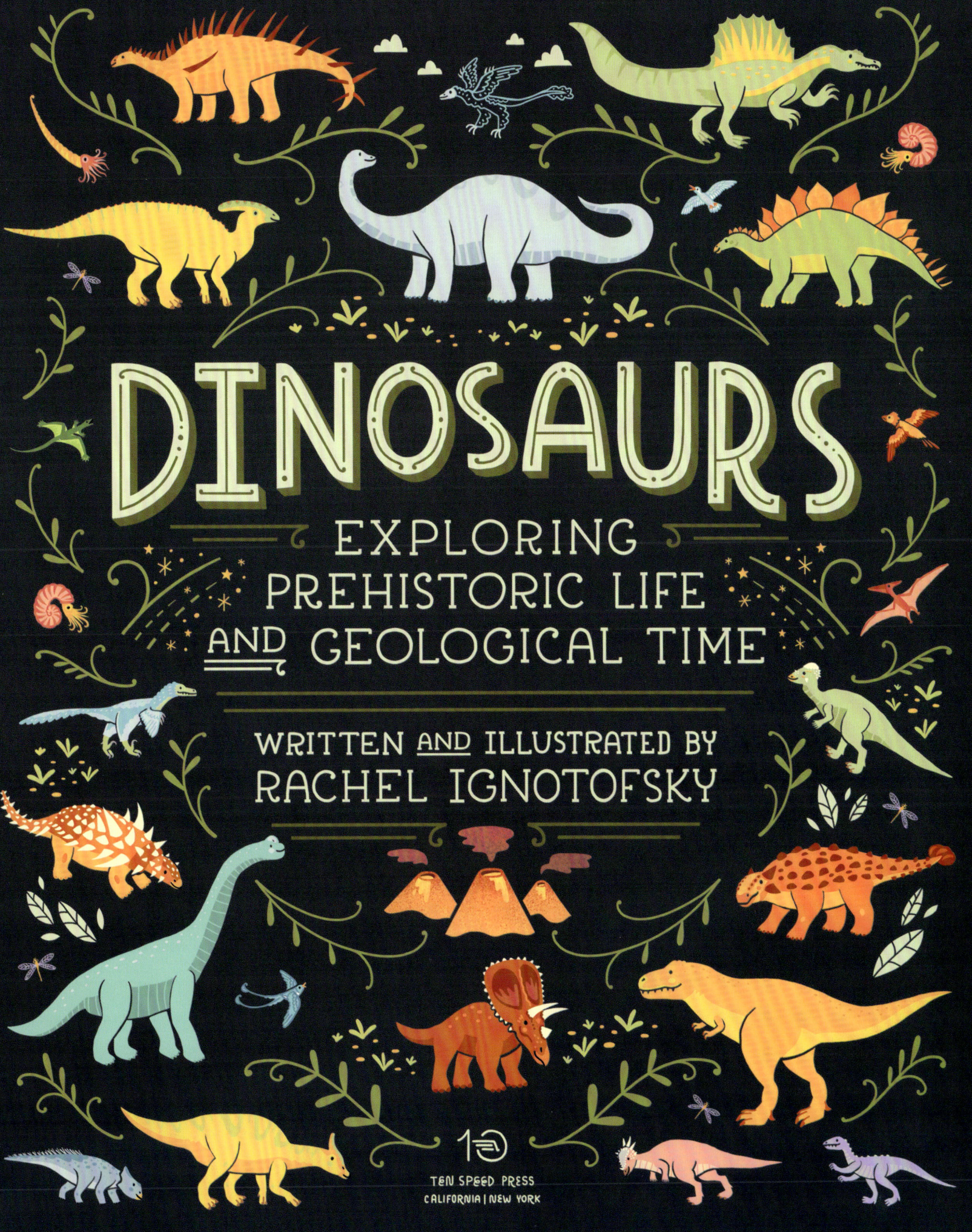

DINOSAURS

EXPLORING PREHISTORIC LIFE AND GEOLOGICAL TIME

WRITTEN AND ILLUSTRATED BY
RACHEL IGNOTOFSKY

TEN SPEED PRESS
CALIFORNIA | NEW YORK

CONTENTS

▼▼▼ YOUNG EARTH AND FIRST LIFE ▼▼▼

▲▲▲ LIFE BEFORE THE DINOSAURS ▲▲▲

AGE OF THE DINOSAURS

MESOZOIC ERA:
252 MYA TO 66 MYA 67

AFTER THE DINOSAURS: RISE OF THE MAMMALS

CENOZOIC ERA:
66 MYA TO TODAY 99

INTRODUCTION

In 1905, the *New York Times* **declared that** "The Tyrant Lizard King" had arrived in Manhattan and "The newly discovered monster was the absolute warlord of the Earth in his day." The bones of the *Tyrannosaurus rex* had been blasted out of rocks in the badlands of Montana by paleontologist Barnum Brown. Shipped by train to New York City, this "monstrous" fossil find was exactly what the American Museum of Natural History needed to draw in crowds.

"THE TYRANT LIZARD KING"

Natural history museums had a lot of competition in the early 1900s. Opulent art museums easily attracted donors, while circus-style cabinets of curiosities could draw rowdy crowds with items such as "mermaids" made of different animal parts sewn together. Around this time, the American Museum of Natural History's attendance had fallen. Dinosaur fossils were both pioneering science and spectacle—the perfect solution to their problems.

In 1906, the first *T. rex* bones went on display—without a head or a tail. Finally, in 1915, the first full *Tyrannosaurus* skeleton was mounted, and the American Museum of Natural History had lines around the block. The *T. rex* towered above the exhibit hall with its voracious jaw and giant teeth. Looking at its ghastly skull, it was obvious why this dinosaur captivated the public. An icon was born, and "dino-mania" took over the world.

1915 *T. REX* CONFIGURATION

MY WORD!

WHAT A BEAST!

HOW GHASTLY!

SWOON

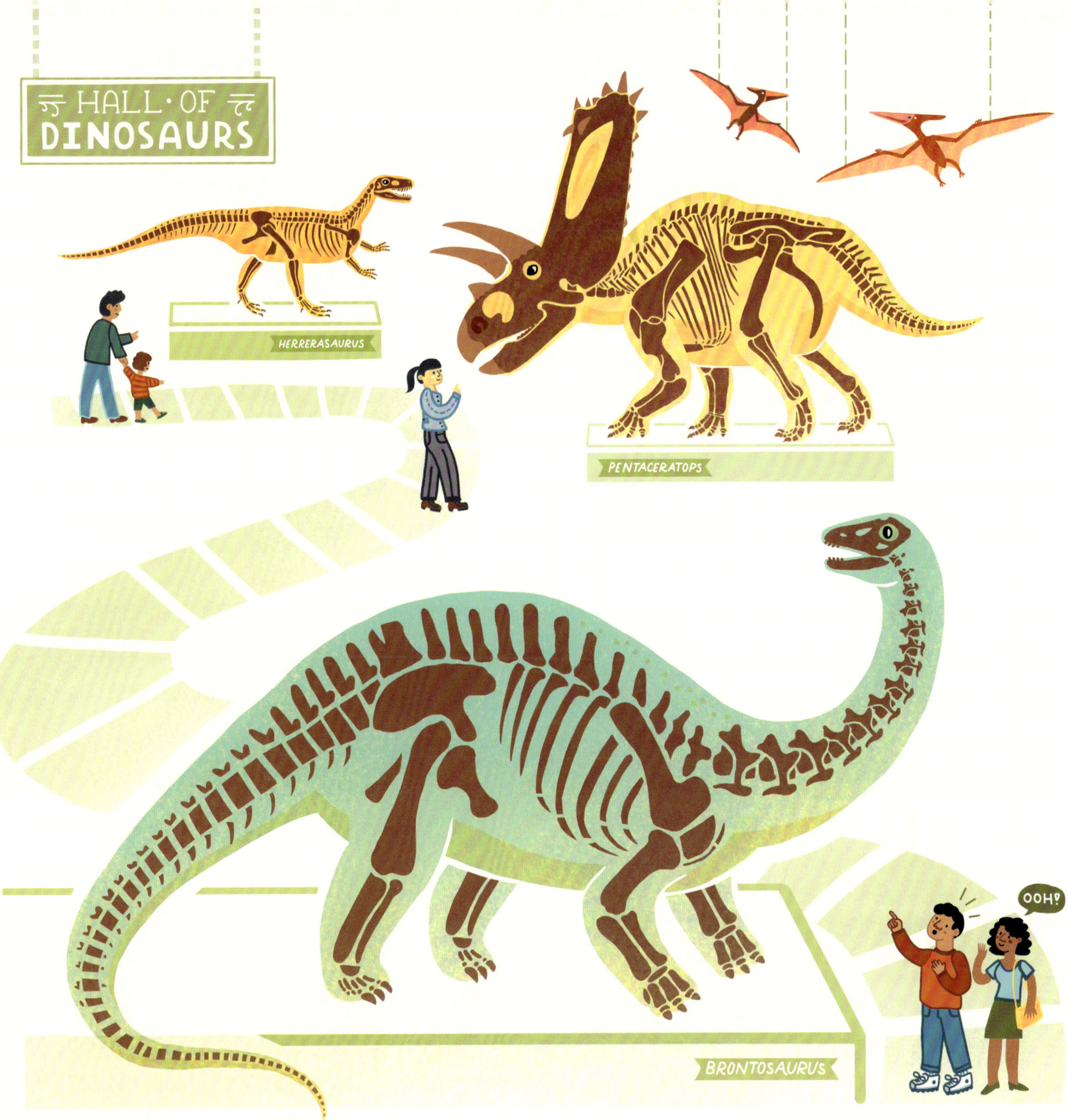
HALL · OF
DINOSAURS
HERRERASAURUS
PENTACERATOPS
BRONTOSAURUS
OOH!

Today, millions visit natural history museums to view the remains of dinosaurs and other prehistoric giants. When standing before the bones of long-extinct animals, you can't help but wonder: How old is the Earth? How has our planet changed? The answers can be found by exploring geological time, using clues like fossils, and analyzing ancient rocks.

This book is not only about ferocious dinosaurs—it is a journey through Earth's more than 4.5-billion-year history. In the grand scheme of deep time, humanity has not been here for very long. By learning about geological time, we can better understand the current chapter of Earth's history and our place in it.

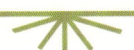

GEOLOGICAL TIME SCALE

Earth is more than 4.5 billion years old, and understanding the magnitude of this kind of "deep time" can be hard. Thankfully, geologists have created a system to break down Earth's long history called the geological time scale. It is organized by giant spans of time called eons that are broken up into smaller units of eras that contain even smaller periods and epochs.

WHEN ARE WE NOW?

We are currently living in the Phanerozoic Eon, the Cenozoic Era, the Quaternary Period, and Holocene Epoch. Around 300,000 years ago, modern humans (*Homo sapiens*) evolved, making our existence only 0.007 percent of Earth history.

Dinosaurs are reptiles that lived during the Mesozoic Era, and they dominated the planet for 165 million years. The two main groups of dinosaurs are called Saurischia and Ornithischia and can be differentiated by their hip bone structure. Dinosaur species were incredibly diverse. Some were small and feathered, others were super muscular and covered in spikes, and some were as tall as a building! Follow the branches of this family tree to see the main groups and subgroups that paleontologists use to categorize dinosaurs.

REPTILE

ARCHOSAURS

RARRR

THE NAME DINOSAUR COMES FROM THE GREEK WORDS FOR "FEARFULLY GREAT LIZARD."

PTEROSAURS
FLYING REPTILES. NOT DINOSAURS.

PSEUDOSUCHIANS
CROCODILES AND THEIR EXTINCT RELATIVES. NOT DINOSAURS.

DINOSAURS

SAURISCHIAN
NAME MEANS "LIZARD HIPPED."

ORNITHISCHIAN
NAME MEANS "BIRD HIPPED," BUT THE RESEMBLANCE IS JUST SUPERFICIAL.

SAUROPODS
ARE LONG-NECKED HERBIVORES.

THEROPODS
ARE TWO LEGGED AND MOSTLY CARNIVORES.

BIRDS ARE IN THE THEROPOD DINOSAUR GROUP!

ALL DINOSAURS LAID EGGS!

ALL DINOSAURS HAD CLAWS AND TAILS!

EXCEPT FOR A FEW SEA BIRDS, ALL DINOSAURS LIVED ON LAND.

THYREOPHORANS

ARE HERBIVORES AND ARMORED.

ANKYLOSAURS
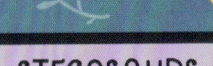
HAVE THICK BODY ARMOR.

STEGOSAURS
HAVE ROWS OF SPIKES.

MARGINOCEPHALIANS

ARE HERBIVORES WITH A BONY SHELF ON BACK OF SKULL.

PACHYCEPHALOSAURS
HAVE THICK SKULLS.

CERATOPSIANS
HAVE FACE HORNS.

ORNITHOPODS

ARE HERBIVORES AND MOSTLY TWO LEGGED.

11

UNDERSTANDING PLATE TECTONICS

Earth's crust is like a giant jigsaw puzzle, made up of humongous slabs of rock called tectonic plates. Slowly, tectonic plates glide along the surface of the planet's mantle. Earth's mantle layer is mostly made of extremely hot, dense, malleable silicate rock. The interaction between tectonic plates spreading out or pushing together causes natural disasters like earthquakes and volcanic eruptions. Plate tectonics are responsible for the movement of continents and the creation of mountain ranges over time.

CONVERGENT PLATE BOUNDARY
▷ PLATES PUSH TOGETHER. ◁

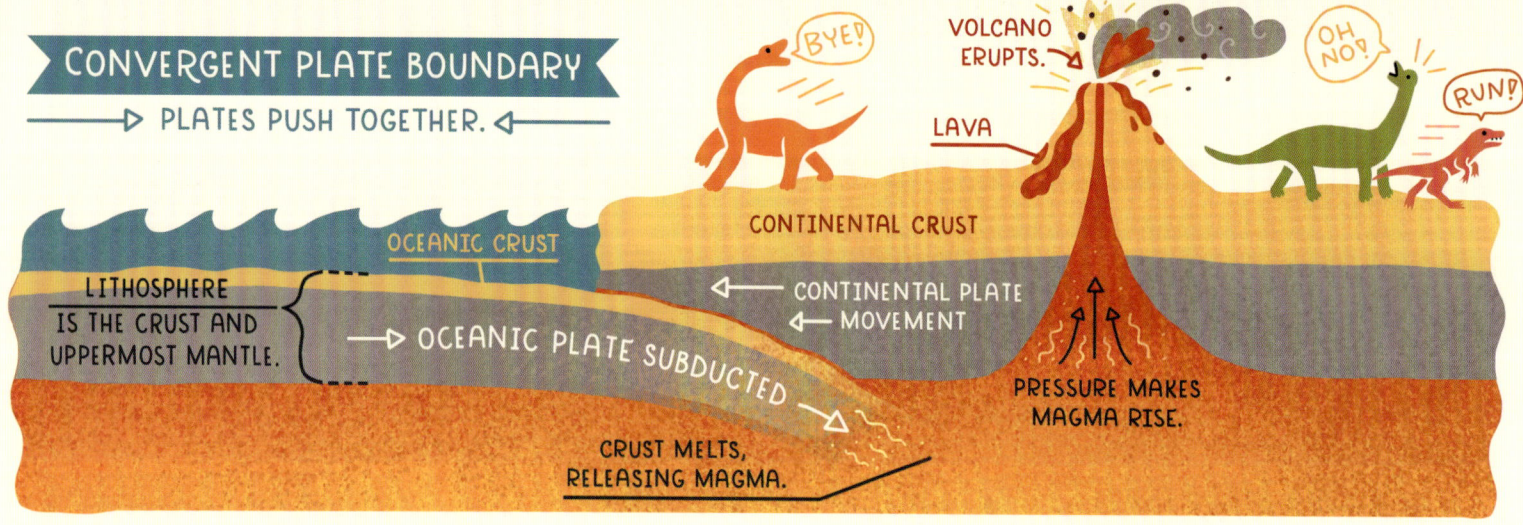

Continental plates are lighter and less dense than oceanic plates. When the two collide, the thinner and heavier oceanic plate is pushed under the continental plate in a process called subduction. With intense heat and pressure, oceanic crust melts down into magma and bubbles up out of the mantle. This new magma rises through the crust, erupting as lava to create volcanoes! When continental plates collide, they can buckle to form mountain ranges.

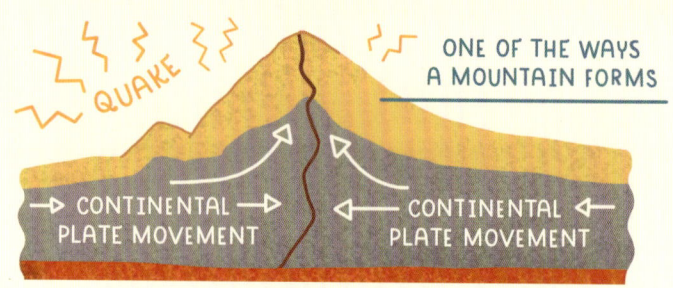

DIVERGENT PLATE BOUNDARY
◁— PLATES MOVE APART. —▷

Deep on the ocean floor, magma from Earth's mantle pushes through the cracks between tectonic plates. This magma cools and forms new crust in a process called seafloor spreading.

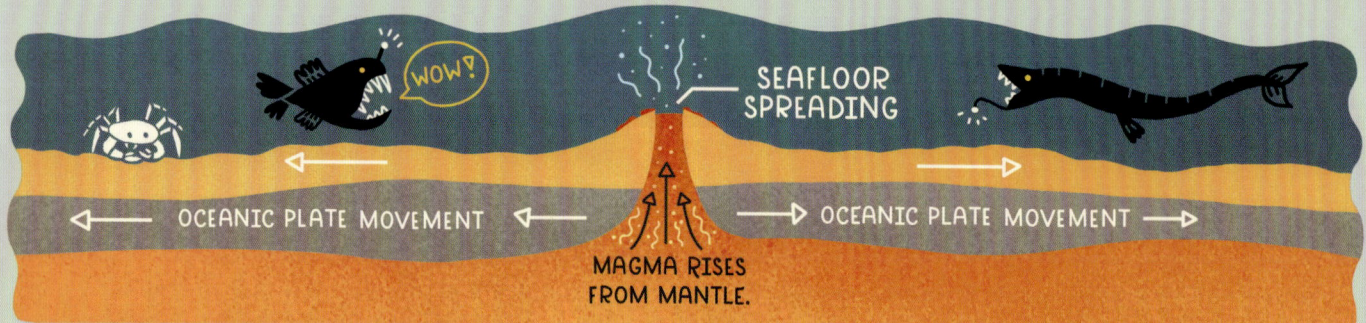

TRANSFORM PLATE BOUNDARY
↖↘ PLATES MOVE SIDE TO SIDE. ↙↗

Most earthquakes are caused by two tectonic plates scraping past each other in opposite directions.

EVER-CHANGING GEOGRAPHY

Plate tectonics mean that Earth's surface is always changing! Right now, the ground beneath our feet is moving about an inch every year. Over long periods of time, the continents have crashed together and drifted apart. The study of Earth's ancient geography is called paleogeography.

AROUND 510 MYA, CAMBRIAN PERIOD

AROUND 430 MYA, SILURIAN PERIOD

AROUND 390 MYA, DEVONIAN PERIOD

AROUND 350 MYA, CARBONIFEROUS PERIOD

AROUND 240 MYA, TRIASSIC PERIOD

AROUND 150 MYA, JURASSIC PERIOD

AROUND 90 MYA, CRETACEOUS PERIOD

TODAY, QUATERNARY PERIOD

WHAT·IS·A· FOSSIL?

Fossils are the remains of long-dead, prehistoric life. Most animals and plants get eaten by scavengers and completely decompose after they die. But under the right circumstances—and with a ton of luck—dead remains can be naturally preserved. For example, fossils have been created when a dead animal (or part of one) is quickly buried under sediment like sand or mud. While the soft tissue decays, hard parts, like bones or shells, are what usually survives to become fossilized. Over a very long time, minerals seep in and slowly replace the organic material until the animal's remains are transformed into stone—forming a preserved fossil.

BODY FOSSILS

These fossils used to be part of a living thing.

SHELL
BONE
LEAF →
EXOSKELETON

TRACE FOSSILS

These fossils are evidence left behind by a living thing.

FOOTPRINTS →
COPROLITE (POOP FOSSIL)

MOLDS AND CASTS

ACTUAL SHELL DISSOLVED!

IMPRESSION LEFT IN ROCK
IMPRESSION FILLED IN

These fossils are impressions left in rock, while the actual specimens have completely dissolved.

UNALTERED PRESERVATION

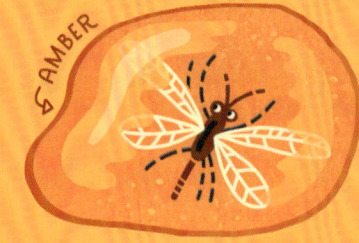

AMBER

In this amber fossil, an entire insect is preserved in crystalized tree sap.

SOFT BODY FOSSILS

OCTOPUS
DINOSAUR SKIN

Preserved soft tissue like this octopus or dinosaur skin is a rare find!

EXAMPLE OF FOSSIL FORMATION:

① BURIAL

SEDIMENT →

A dead *Triceratops* has sunk down to the bottom of a river. It is covered by mud.

② DECAY

Most soft tissue rots away, while hard tissue like bone remains.

③ SEDIMENT BUILDUP

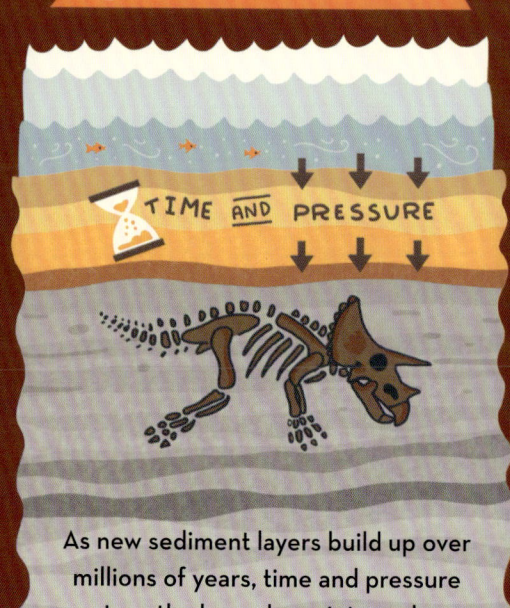

TIME AND PRESSURE

As new sediment layers build up over millions of years, time and pressure turn the lower layer into rock.

READING·THE
ROCKS

Geologists and paleontologists study our planet by looking at rock layers called strata. Strata builds up over millions of years and can be seen as colorful stripes in many rock formations, like the Grand Canyon in Arizona. Generally, the deeper the rock is, the older the strata are, but erosion, earthquakes, and the movement of tectonic plates change the landscape and expose ancient rocks. By comparing rock layers all over the globe and the common fossils found in them, paleontologists can piece together a prehistoric puzzle!

SEDIMENTARY ROCK

CLAY
SHALE
LIMESTONE

Sedimentary rocks are where most fossils are found.

IGNEOUS ROCK

OBSIDIAN
GRANITE

Igneous rocks are the best for radiometric dating.

INDEX FOSSIL

A fossil of a distinct species that was very abundant during a specific range in geological time. Finding one can help date an entire rock formation!

I'M FROM THE CRETACEOUS?

SCAPHITE

RADIOACTIVE ATOMS DECAY.

LOSES PARTICLES

BYE?

RADIOMETRIC DATING:

Scientists use the natural decay of radioactive elements to date ancient rocks and fossils, a process known as radiometric dating! Everything in the universe is made of atoms. Radioactive atoms are unstable and decay over time at a measurable, steady rate. This rate of decay is called a half-life and is nature's hidden clock. Radioactive elements like uranium are found in the crystals of rocks. Using radiometric dating, scientists can determine exactly how old a rock and surrounding fossils are!

④ REPLACEMENT

PRESSURE
MINERALS

The dinosaur remains turn to rock. Chemicals and mineral salts from the water slowly seep in and replace the body's organic tissue, until it transforms into stone. This type of preservation is called mineralization.

⑤ ROCK FORMATION

Over millions of years, more rock layers form and continents move.

⑥ FOSSIL EXPOSED

As even more time goes by, erosion and plate tectonics bring the fossil back to the surface.

MASS EXTINCTION EVENTS

Extinction occurs when a species completely dies out. There are many ways to go extinct. For example, a species can be outcompeted for resources, die out from disease, or have its habitat destroyed. Extinction is a natural part of evolution. More than 99 percent of the species that have ever existed on Earth are now extinct. A mass extinction event is when catastrophe strikes and 75 percent (or more) of all life on Earth dies out within a relatively short period of geological time. There have been five major mass extinctions over the past 538 million years.

···445 MYA TO 443 MYA···

LATE ORDOVICIAN MASS EXTINCTION EVENTS

Scientists theorize that two different waves of dramatic climate change caused species to die out. First, a global ice age caused ocean levels to fall, which led to the destruction of warm-water habitats. This was followed by a period of increased greenhouse gases like carbon dioxide in the atmosphere, which caused global warming. The oceans became oxygen-depleted with toxic levels of sulfide.

ABOUT **85%** OF ALL ANIMAL SPECIES EXTINCT

···372 MYA TO 359 MYA···

LATE DEVONIAN MASS EXTINCTION EVENT

This mass extinction is still a big mystery. The fossil record shows a steady drop-off in new species over millions of years and a depletion of oxygen in the oceans. Researchers debate the cause—theories include global warming being caused by undersea volcanoes, or an out-of-control algae bloom, or even an asteroid impact.

ABOUT **75%** OF ALL ANIMAL SPECIES EXTINCT

···252 MYA···

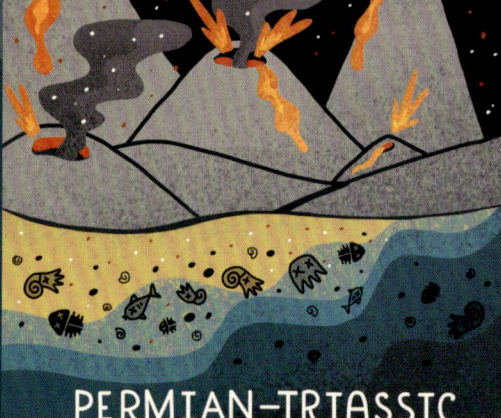

PERMIAN-TRIASSIC MASS EXTINCTION EVENT

Called the Great Dying, there is still debate over the cause of Earth's worst mass extinction event. Most scientists think it was triggered by huge volcanic eruptions in what is now Siberia. Volcanic outgassing of greenhouse gasses like carbon dioxide may have caused catastrophic global warming, where the oceans became acidic, depleted of oxygen, and filled with toxic sulfides. An asteroid hit Earth around this time, causing a 25-mile-wide crater in Brazil, which possibly added to the ongoing climate disaster.

ABOUT **90%** OF ALL ANIMAL SPECIES EXTINCT

OVER 99% OF THE SPECIES THAT HAVE EVER EXISTED ON EARTH ARE NOW EXTINCT.

TRILOBITES
—R.I.P.—

R.I.P. T. REX

THE DODO
—R.I.P.—

201 MYA

TRIASSIC–JURASSIC MASS EXTINCTION EVENT

The shifting of tectonic plates caused massive volcanic eruptions. The volcanic outgassing of greenhouse gasses like carbon dioxide caused global temperatures to steadily rise and the oceans to acidify. This extinction event paved the way for dinosaurs to become Earth's dominant species for the rest of the Mesozoic Era.

ABOUT **76%** OF ALL ANIMAL SPECIES EXTINCT

66 MYA

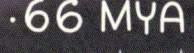

CRETACEOUS–PALEOGENE MASS EXTINCTION EVENT

A giant asteroid crashed into Earth, causing a 112-mile-wide impact crater in Mexico. Shockwaves were felt around the world. Debris shot up into space and reentered Earth's atmosphere at high speeds, raining down millions of tiny glass balls that super-heated the air. Wildfires engulfed the planet, and soot blocked out the sun. All non-avian dinosaurs went extinct.

ABOUT **80%** OF ALL ANIMAL SPECIES EXTINCT

LIFE BOUNCES BACK.

Earth's history is long and ever changing, and life has bounced back after every mass extinction, even if it takes a long time. Survivors find themselves in a world with way less competition. As new ecosystems emerge, many new species rapidly evolve in an empty playing field. This process is called adaptive radiation.

UNDERSTANDING EVOLUTION

Evolution is the process of genetic change over multiple generations. It is how life adapts and reacts to an ever-changing environment and allows for the creation of new species. All life on Earth evolved from the very first simple single-celled organisms. Billions of years and countless generations later, evolution has allowed for an abundance of complex life-forms to flourish on this little space rock we call home.

SPECIES:
A specific type of living thing. Individuals of the same species can reproduce together and create fertile offspring.

DNA (Deoxyribonucleic Acid):
Deoxyribonucleic acid is a long molecule inside a cell that carries the genetic information that acts as a set of instructions. When cells reproduce, DNA splits in half to copy itself.

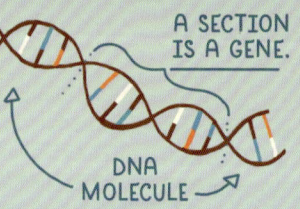

A SECTION IS A GENE.

DNA MOLECULE

HEREDITY:
Parents pass down their genes (made up of DNA) to their offspring during reproduction. Genes are inherited in different combinations, causing variation of traits between siblings.

DOG PARENTS

PUPPIES

VARIATION IN SIBLINGS

MUTATION:
Random changes and errors can happen when DNA replicates. This random change in the genetic code can cause slight differences between members of the same species. Neutral or beneficial changes can be passed down to the next generation.

NATURAL SELECTION:
Individuals of the same species have slight differences! Certain variations and beneficial traits can help one survive danger or outcompete others for resources. Living things that are better suited to their environment will likely have more chances to reproduce and pass down these traits to the next generation.

I'M HUNGRY!

GIRAFFES WITH LONGER NECKS OUTCOMPETE OTHERS FOR FOOD.

LONG-NECKED GIRAFFES REPRODUCE MORE.

OVER GENERATIONS, ALL GIRAFFES HAVE LONG NECKS.

MICROEVOLUTION:
Over a few generations, species adapt to better survive in their environment, changing their appearance or abilities.

YUM!

OH NO!

I'M HIDDEN NOW?

OH NO!

SOME PEPPERED MOTHS BLEND IN BETTER WITH WHITE BIRCH TREES.

IN THE 1800S, COAL POLLUTION SUDDENLY TURNED TREES BLACK.

IN ONLY A FEW GENERATIONS, PEPPERED MOTHS EVOLVED TO BLEND IN WITH THEIR NEW ENVIRONMENT.

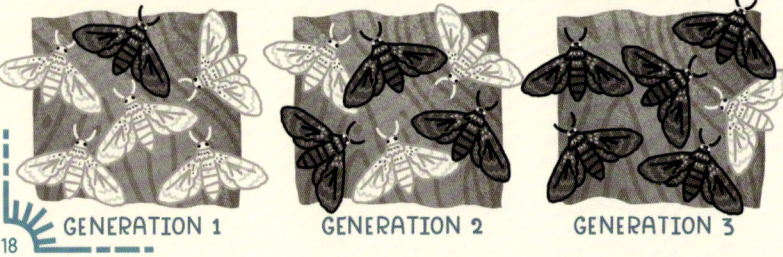

GENERATION 1

GENERATION 2

GENERATION 3

MACROEVOLUTION:
Over long periods of time, small changes can add up until a completely new species emerges. On a large scale, this explains brand-new types of life, with new body plans and abilities. Over billions of years, this is how single-celled organisms evolved into complex animals.

EVOLUTIONARY ANCESTORS OF A MODERN WHALE

PAKICETUS, 50 MYA

AMBULOCETUS, 49 MYA

BASILOSAURUS, 35 MYA

I'VE CHANGED A LOT OVER MILLENNIA?

MODERN WHALES, 34 MYA–NOW

CONVERGENT EVOLUTION:

When two unrelated species independently evolve a similar body plan. Even though they look the same, they did not inherit their traits from a common ancestor. Instead, the two species adapted in reaction to similar environmental pressures.

ICHTHYOSAUR, A MARINE REPTILE

DOLPHIN, A MARINE MAMMAL

ALLOPATRIC SPECIATION:

Mountain ranges, rivers, canyons, and oceans are all physical barriers that can isolate plants and animals. When members of the same species are separated by a geographical barrier for a long period of time, they can evolve into completely different species from one another.

STEM VERSUS CROWN GROUPS:

Evolution is messy. To keep track of how species are related, scientists have created a complex branching family tree that maps out the relationships of everything that has ever lived.

CROWN GROUP:

All descendants of the last common ancestor of a living group, extinct or alive.

STEM GROUPS:

Made up only of extinct animals. Although stem groups share many traits with the crown group, they are evolutionary cousins and not directly related to the modern living species. Their lineage branched off earlier from a common stem. Fossils from stem species give us insight into missing links that have not been found yet.

STEM GROUP

ARCHAEOPTERYX

AVES

LIVING BIRDS

CROWN GROUP

ARCHAEOPTERYX IS A BIRDLIKE DINOSAUR BUT IS NOT DIRECTLY RELATED TO THE ANCESTOR OF ALL LIVING BIRDS.

STORIES OF DISCOVERY:

Evolution is a unifying scientific theory that was explained in the late 1850s by two British naturalists, Charles Darwin and Alfred Russel Wallace. Each independently observed the diversity and adaptations of animals on their travels.

Famously, Darwin traveled to the Galapagos Islands. He noticed the different beak shapes of the various species of finches that lived on different islands, with each beak best suited for the specific environment. He concluded that the finches all had a common ancestor, from which they evolved in reaction to their unique surroundings. Wallace came to the same conclusion while studying monkeys in the Amazon. Since the mid-1800s, countless experiments, observations, and rigorous research have proven the theory of evolution!

COMMON ANCESTOR

COMMON CACTUS FINCH

EATS CACTUS

LARGE GROUND FINCH

EATS SEEDS

GRAY WARBLER-FINCH

EATS INSECTS

"FROM SO SIMPLE A BEGINNING, ENDLESS FORMS MOST BEAUTIFUL AND MOST WONDERFUL HAVE BEEN AND ARE BEING EVOLVED." —CHARLES DARWIN

YOUNG EARTH AND FIRST·LIFE

PROTEROZOIC EARTH

PRECAMBRIAN·SUPEREON
OVER 4567 MILLION YEARS TO 538.8 MILLION YEARS AGO

For most of Earth's history, the planet was an inhospitable ball of barren rock and water, where life could only exist as simple single-celled organisms. The Precambrian Supereon made up the first 4 billion years of our planet's existence. This unfathomable stretch of time tells the story of how Earth formed in the chaos of the young solar system and how it dramatically transformed into a place where life could thrive.

Studying rocks from the Precambrian Supereon is difficult. Time and pressure over billions of years have taken a toll on the clues that scientists need. Most ancient rocks have eroded into sand or melted when pushed down toward Earth's fiery mantle, leaving very little fossil record of this time. In the past, a majority of scientists took this lack of fossil evidence as proof that it was impossible for large, complex life-forms to have existed during the Precambrian Supereon. But in the 1950s, a group of British teenagers playing in their local forest stumbled upon a 570-million-year-old fossil discovery that would change everything. The rocks were covered in the imprints of pillowy animals that looked like ferns. That was just the start of new discoveries!

At the very end of the Precambrian Supereon, the oceans contained bizarre ecosystems of slow-moving, living blobs that slid across the ocean floor grazing on algae, while fields of coral-like animals waved in the water. It is hard to see how these ancient life-forms, without mouths or eyes, relate to modern animals or even plants. It took life billions of years to jump from a single cell to something resembling a jellyfish. And as far as we know, it has only happened on Earth.

GEOLOGICAL TIME SCALE

OVER 4567 MYA	4031 MYA	2500 MYA	538.8 MYA	NOW

PRECAMBRIAN SUPEREON			PHANEROZOIC EON
HADEAN EON	ARCHEAN EON	PROTEROZOIC EON	

21

THE HADEAN EON

Seas of lava, meteors crashing down from the sky, a burning lifeless planet—welcome to young Earth. More than 4.5 billion years ago, our solar system began as dust and rocks swirling around a newly formed sun. Large asteroids and ice clumped together, drawn by each other's gravitational forces, forming planets. As Earth grew, so did its gravitational pull. In the crowded early solar system, asteroids, comets, and meteors constantly smacked into Earth, which both added to its size and super-heated its surface. Scientists estimate that Earth formed more than 4.567 billion years ago. Millions of years later, the constant meteor bombardment stopped, which allowed Earth to slowly cool and form a crust and atmosphere.

FORMATION OF THE EARTH

① ② ③ ④

Earth's first atmosphere was practically nonexistent, composed of helium and hydrogen that instantly released into space. Luckily, Hadean Earth was covered in nonstop volcanic eruptions that spewed greenhouse gasses, like carbon dioxide and nitrogen. These gasses reshaped Earth's atmosphere into a stable layer that protected it from outer space. Scientists theorize that volcanoes also released water vapor that created Earth's first oceans. Exactly how Earth's oceans formed is still a mystery.

FUN FACTS:

During this eon, the moon was about fifteen times closer to Earth.

HI?

LOOKS LIKE HOME TO ME!

The Hadean Eon is named after Hades, the Greek god of the Underworld.

Hadean Earth rotated faster than it does now and had a 6-hour day. Earth's rotation slows about 1.8 milliseconds every 100 years because of the gravitational pull of our moon.

EARTH TODAY

OUTER CORE

INNER CORE

CRUST

MANTLE

Earth's crust is only 1 percent of the entire planet and, on dry land, averages 25 miles deep.

STORIES OF DISCOVERY:

Erosion, volcanoes, and tectonic activity have destroyed nearly every Earth rock left from the Hadean Eon. The ones that do exist are highly compressed minerals and crystals. The best leftovers from the Hadean are meteors and the moon itself! Apollo 14 was the United States's third trip to the moon's surface. Although this 1971 expedition became famous for astronaut Alan Shepard's lunar golfing, the real accomplishment was bringing home over 243 pounds of moon rocks! By examining samples like these and analyzing a crystalized mineral in moon rocks called zircon, scientists dated the moon at 4.46 billion years old. A mainstream theory is that the moon formed after a small planet named Theia crashed into Earth. This caused massive amounts of debris from both planets to become stuck in Earth's orbit, which converged to create our moon.

FORMATION OF THE MOON

① THEIA EARTH ② ③ DEBRIS TRAPPED IN EARTH'S ORBIT EARTH ④ EARTH MOON

Archean Earth might as well have been an alien world. It was a ball of scorching-hot water and toxic air. With hardly any land, the planet was covered in oceans twice as salty as they are today. There was zero breathable oxygen, and the atmosphere was entirely made of greenhouse gasses like methane and carbon dioxide. (These gasses get their nickname because they lock in heat, just like the reflective glass greenhouses that are used to create controlled warm environments in gardens.) Archean Earth was sweltering! Global temperatures reached anywhere from 131 to 176°F.

Earth's first life-forms were heat-loving, extremely simple, and durable microorganisms called prokaryotes. Deep in the dark ocean, these microbes did not need oxygen or light. Instead, chemicals that spewed from undersea volcanic vents powered these single-celled microbes. Evidence of microscopic prokaryote fossils that are 3.49 billion years old have been found in South Africa and Western Australia.

There had to be an easier way of getting energy than clinging to heat vents. What about the sun, the giant nuclear reactor in the sky? Cyanobacteria, a different kind of prokaryote, evolved a way to "eat" the sun's solar energy in a process called photosynthesis (just like how today's plants make energy). During photosynthesis, carbon dioxide is absorbed from the atmosphere and oxygen is released as waste. Around 2.4 billion years ago, cyanobacteria dominated the shallow waters of our planet. As they devoured carbon dioxide, the microbes outgassed oxygen on a grand scale, thus starting the Great Oxygenation Event, which marked the end of the Archean Eon and paved the way for complex life-forms to evolve.

FUN FACTS:

It is hypothesized that Earth's first continent, named "Ur," emerged above the ocean around 3 billion years ago.

KOMATI FORMATION, 3.5-BILLION-YEAR-OLD VOLCANIC ROCK

The Komati River valley in South Africa has some of the oldest-surviving rocks on Earth!

LAVA MOON?

The large dark spots on the moon called the Lunar Mare were created during intense volcanic eruptions from 3800 mya to 3000 mya.

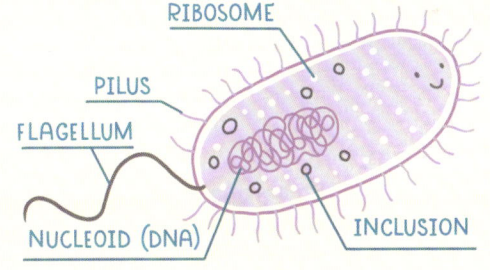

RIBOSOME

PILUS

FLAGELLUM

NUCLEOID (DNA)

INCLUSION

Prokaryotes were the earliest type of life on Earth. They are so simple that they have no nucleus or mitochondria.

STORIES OF DISCOVERY:

TODAY'S LIVING STROMATOLITES

FOSSILIZED STROMATOLITES

If you visit the shallow waters of Western Australia, you can see stromatolites, a living fossil. What appear to be pillowy rocks are actually microbial mats, large colonies of single-celled bacteria. Today, the stromatolites living in Australia are made up of cyanobacteria and are thought to be identical to structures from billions of years ago. Their fossils leave behind a distinct crinkled layered pattern in the rocks. The oldest stromatolite fossil has been dated at 3.45 billion years old, pushing back scientists' theories on when the first photosynthesizing cyanobacteria developed. Records of Archean life are incredibly hard to find, mainly because so few rocks remain from that time. Exactly what the Archean world looked like is still a big mystery.

The Proterozoic Eon was a time of many firsts: the first mega continent, the first ice age, even the first animals! What kicks off this eon is the Great Oxygenation Event, caused by the waste buildup of photosynthesizing cyanobacteria. This was the first time that Earth was transformed by the actions of a living thing. For more than 300 million years, oxygen slowly built up. Breathable oxygen is a good fuel for cells and is necessary for complex life-forms to evolve. Around 1900 mya, eukaryotes evolved as the first complex single-celled life-form containing a nucleus. Today, all animals, plants, protists, and fungi are made up of eukaryotic cells.

Geologists have found clues of Earth's first ice age all around the world in the form of drop stones, which are "out of place" rocks left behind by melting glaciers. This evidence has led many scientists to propose a controversial Snowball Earth or Slush Ball Earth theory. No one knows exactly why the climate changed during the ice age, but many scientists propose that the atmosphere lost its warming greenhouse gasses when oceanwide algae blooms released too much oxygen. According to the theory, Earth was heavily glaciated—possibly to the equator—and almost all life died except the most resilient microbes. Suddenly, the earth warmed until even the ice caps completely melted. Scientists hypothesize that a combination of volcanic activity and the lack of algae allowed greenhouse gasses to return and balance out the atmosphere.

At the very end of the Proterozoic Eon, during the Ediacaran Period (635 mya to 538.8 mya), Earth experienced its most exciting change: the first large multicellular animals evolved! Earth's warm oceans filled with sponges, slow-moving blobs, and animals that looked like strange plants. The stage was set for an explosion of underwater life!

FUN FACTS:

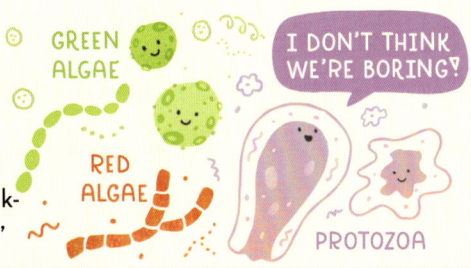

Between 1.8 billion and 0.8 billion years ago, life and climate on Earth were so stable, this period is nicknamed "the boring billion."

GREEN ALGAE
RED ALGAE
I DON'T THINK WE'RE BORING!
PROTOZOA

By the Proterozoic Eon, Earth had cooled enough for modern plate tectonics to form continents and mountain ranges.

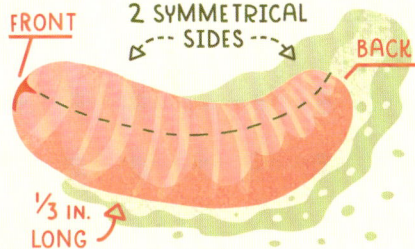

Ikaria wariootia (555 mya) is the one of the earliest-known bilaterian animals with a clear front and back. This body plan would dominate the animal world!

FRONT
2 SYMMETRICAL SIDES
BACK
⅓ IN. LONG

AN ANCIENT RELATIVE TO ANEMONES, CORALS, AND JELLYFISH

Auroralumina (560 mya) had tentacles to catch prey, making it one of the oldest-known predators.

STORIES OF DISCOVERY:

TEXTURE RUBBING

CHARNIA FOSSILS HAVE BEEN FOUND THAT ARE OVER 6 FT. TALL!

The Charnwood Forest of England is one of the best places to find fossils from the Late Proterozoic Eon. For a very long time, geologists thought that no multicellular life existed before the Cambrian Period (538.8 mya). In 1956, a 15-year-old girl named Tina Negus came across unusual fernlike patterns in the 570-million-year-old rocks in Charnwood. Sadly, Tina's findings were dismissed by her teacher as a mistake. The next year, three teenage boys also found fossils in Charnwood while rock climbing. One of them was Roger Mason, who convinced his father's friend and geologist, Trevor Ford, to visit the site. Ford was shocked—this find would change everything! He removed the fossils, which he named *Charnia*, for further study and soon published the findings. Although *Charnia* looked like a quilted puffy fern, it was actually an animal. With no mouth or guts, it lived anchored to the ocean floor and passively absorbed nutrients that floated by. Discoveries at Charnwood Forest sparked a reexamination of previously mislabeled or dismissed fossils around the world. The Ediacaran Period at the end of the Proterozoic Eon was teeming with animals!

CAMBRIAN EARTH ⬆

SILURIAN EARTH

ORDOVICIAN EARTH →

DEVONIAN EARTH →

CARBONIFEROUS EARTH ⬆

PERMIAN EARTH →

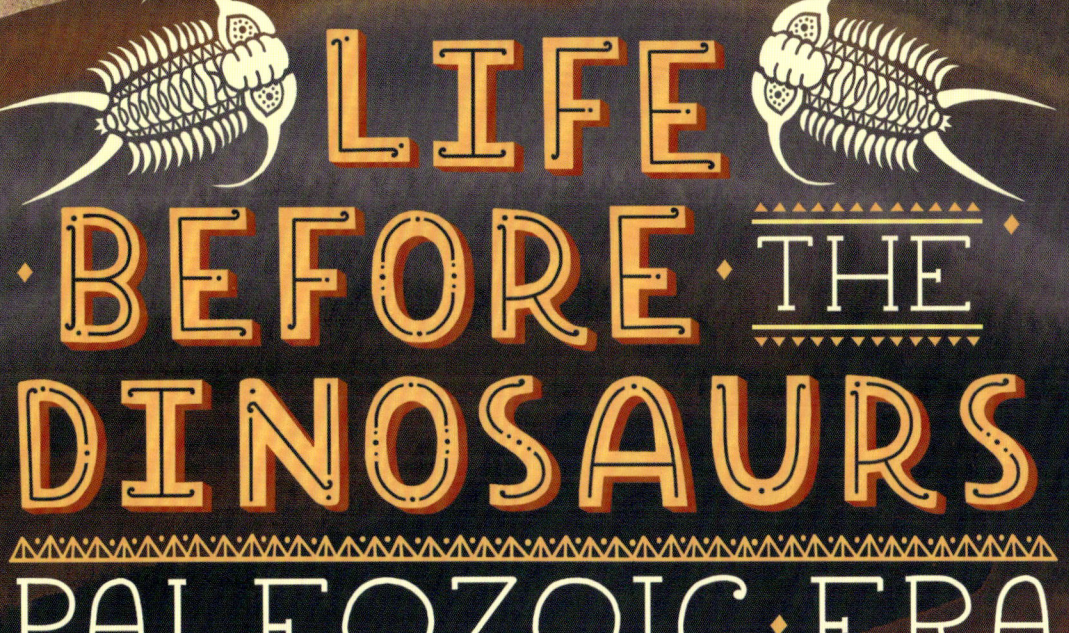

LIFE BEFORE THE DINOSAURS

PALEOZOIC · ERA

538.8 MILLION YEARS TO 252 MILLION YEARS AGO

During the Paleozoic Era, life left the oceans to colonize dry land and even take to the sky. The immensely long Precambrian Supereon came to an end with an evolutionary event known as the Cambrian Explosion, which littered the fossil record with exciting new life-forms. Before this, the fossil record contained Ediacaran sluggish blobs and completely motionless animals like *Charnia*. Suddenly there was an abundance of sea life that crawled, wiggled, and swam.

It is during the six geological periods that make up the Paleozoic Era when life evolved its first backbone, first lungs, and first legs. Plants, starting as little more than pond scum, evolved into massive trees and continent-spanning forests. Arthropods that first scuttled around on the ocean floor eventually crawled out of the sea. Insects developed wings to become Earth's first fliers. Soft-bodied vertebrate fishes kept adapting until they could survive on dry land. Vertebrates eventually grew so large that they became the first megafauna to roam the landscape.

The Paleozoic Era was bookended by the most devastating mass extinction event in Earth's history. Despite the many species that were lost, the survivors proved that the body plans developed during this long era were evolutionary winners. Eyes, mouths, legs, lungs, fins, and wings are just some of the legacies that the Paleozoic left behind.

GEOLOGICAL TIME SCALE

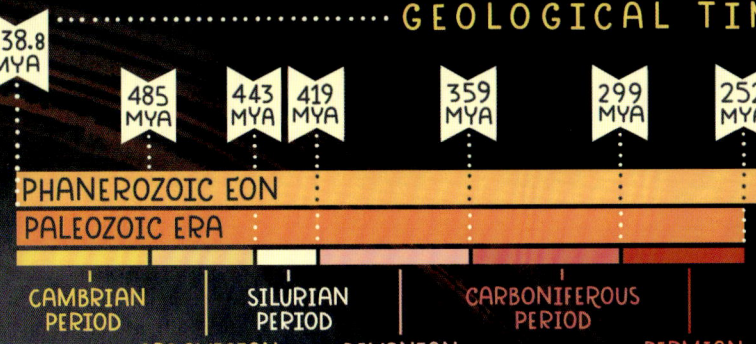

538.8 MYA · 485 MYA · 443 MYA · 419 MYA · 359 MYA · 299 MYA · 252 MYA · NOW

PHANEROZOIC EON

PALEOZOIC ERA

CAMBRIAN PERIOD

ORDOVICIAN PERIOD

SILURIAN PERIOD

DEVONIAN PERIOD

CARBONIFEROUS PERIOD

PERMIAN PERIOD

ANOMALOCARIS

VETULICOLA
CUNEATA

MYLLOKUNMINGIA FENGJIAOA

ISOXYS
ACUTANGULUS

COTYLEDION
TYLODES

ONYCHODICTYON FEROX

SPONGE

THE CAMBRIAN PERIOD

538.8 MILLION YEARS TO 485 MILLION YEARS AGO

Something dramatically changed in the ocean's ecosystems 538.8 mya. Gone were the sleepy and slow-moving communities of Ediacaran animals. What replaced them in a span of a few million years was a chaotic frenzy of new organisms. This explosion of biodiversity was caused by a rapid increase of oxygen in the atmosphere and the evolution of predators. The new life-forms of the Cambrian developed complex muscle fibers, nerves, and eyeballs that could form images in a brain. To support all this new activity, these animals needed a cellular fuel source more efficient than carbon dioxide. They needed oxygen!

The Cambrian Explosion was a spike in biodiversity that the planet had never seen before! Although different factors could have caused this change, many scientists think a boom in oxygen is one of the major causes. Oxygen released as a byproduct of microbial photosynthesis had built up in the atmosphere over millions of years. This gas had a great effect on Earth's crust in a process called oxidation. This chemical weathering process slowly breaks down rocks, freeing the calcium and phosphorus inside them and allowing these minerals to enter the oceans. Calcium and phosphorus are important building blocks for complex animal life.

Life-forms now scurried, burrowed, and powerfully swam through the ocean. Animals developed pincers, claws, hardened calcium plates to repel attacks, and multiple eyeballs on stalks in an evolutionary arms race to conquer the seas.

XIANGUANGIA SINICA

EOREDLICHIA

THE CAMBRIAN PERIOD
LAND AND SEA

While life on land was completely barren during the Cambrian Period, in the oceans it was the age of the arthropods! Arthropods are animals with exoskeletons and jointed legs. Today, arthropods make up 75 percent of animal life on Earth and include familiar critters like insects, spiders, and crustaceans. A segmented body plan made of armored plates was a winning combination for many animals during the Cambrian. For example, *Marrella*, a bug-like creature nicknamed the lace crab, is one of the most common fossils from this time. Swarms of tiny trilobites stampeded across the sun-drenched shallow seabed, chased by giant shrimp-like *Anomalocaris*. Cambrian arthropods were on the move and had many features of modern animals!

Meanwhile, among the blooms of jellyfishes and fields of seaweed, a rare, tiny, soft-bodied creature had a new feature inside its body: a primitive spinal cord! Around 530 mya, fish-like animals, like *Pikaia*, had bodies supported by a thin flexible rod with a long nerve called a notochord. Cambrian animals like these are considered the earliest ancestors of all animals with spines, including humans. These inch-long, squishy swimmers managed to survive natural selection's first gauntlet, up against hungry, hard-shelled, pinching arthropods. Had animals like *Pikaia* met an unlucky end this far back in time, maybe today's Earth would be a crab-dominated world out of science fiction!

FUN FACTS:

Arthropods in the genus *Opabinia* had five eyeballs and a proboscis. Nature was experimenting!

Animals like *Banffia* are from a mysterious phylum called Vetulicolia that went extinct 500 mya. They were free-swimming filter feeders that looked like tadpoles.

The first cephalopod, *Plectronoceras*, evolved in the Late Cambrian. Only the shell is fossilized.

DID IT HAVE TENTACLES OR WAS IT LIKE A SNAIL?

Hallucigenia was discovered in 1911, but it took 80 years for paleontologists to decide which side of the animal was the feet.

STORIES OF DISCOVERY:

The Canadian Burgess Shale, discovered by rail workers in 1886, is one of the best-preserved fossil beds in the world. Situated at an elevation of 7,500 feet in the Canadian Rockies, the exposed rock contains the fossils of many animals from the Middle Cambrian Period. For reasons not entirely known, the fine mud of the shale preserved the soft body parts of animals that are almost never fossilized, like worms and jellyfishes. Ordinarily, bacteria and fungi decompose dead organisms, leaving only shells or bones to be fossilized. In the Burgess Shale, an entire ecosystem of animals who had been going about their business 509 mya was discovered frozen in rock.

The diversity of animals was unheard of from such ancient rocks! Between 1909 and 1924, the head of the Smithsonian Institution, Charles Walcott, led excavations of the Burgess Shale that revealed more than 60,000 fossils. The high quality of specimens discovered filled in an evolutionary gap in the fossil record that had bothered biologists, including Charles Darwin. The Burgess Shale has been an active dig site for more than 100 years, and it still produces new species. It can be visited by the public on guided tours through Yoho National Park!

··THE CAMBRIAN PERIOD··
CREATURE FEATURE

ASAPHISCUS
ARTHROPODA
MIDDLE CAMBRIAN
3 IN. LONG

TRILOBITES ARE THE →
ONLY ANIMALS TO
HAVE CRYSTAL EYES
MADE OF CALCITE.

TRILOBITE MEANS
"THREE LOBES"
IN LATIN.

PARADOXIDES
ARTHROPODA
MIDDLE CAMBRIAN
17 ½ IN. LONG

TRILOBITES FILL THE
ECOLOGICAL NICHE
THAT CRABS AND
LOBSTERS DO TODAY.

TRILOBITES THROUGHOUT TIME:

These little arthropods are one of the most successful animal classes of all time. For 270 million years—longer than dinosaurs and birds have existed—trilobites lived in the oceans and saw quite a lot. Trilobites look like pill bugs and are a common fossil from the Cambrian Period. Since they shed a hard exoskeleton with each growth spurt, many of the fossils are just cast-off trilobite armor, rather than the animal itself. Some trilobites were fast swimmers in the upper water column like today's sardines, but most contented themselves to live on the bottom of the ocean.

As strange as these animals may seem, the Cambrian marks the first point in the fossil record where we can see a bit of ourselves. Trilobites have a head at the front of their body with two eyes and a mouth underneath. (Sounds familiar!) Looking at a trilobite fossil 500 million years later, this is an

TRILOBITES WERE
FIRST WRITTEN
ABOUT IN 1698.

instantly recognizable body plan that is shared across deep time. By the end of the Paleozoic Era, the last species of trilobites were only a few centimeters long. The last of them died in the Permian-Triassic mass extinction event, bringing the trilobites' long saga to an end.

TRILOBITES ACROSS THE PALEOZOIC ERA

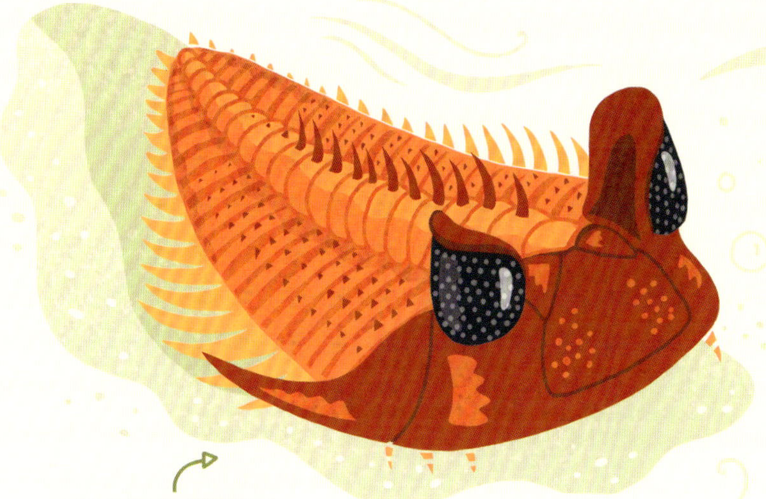

ERBENOCHILE

EARLY TO MIDDLE DEVONIAN
2 IN. LONG

ASAPHUS

MIDDLE ORDOVICIAN
3 IN. LONG

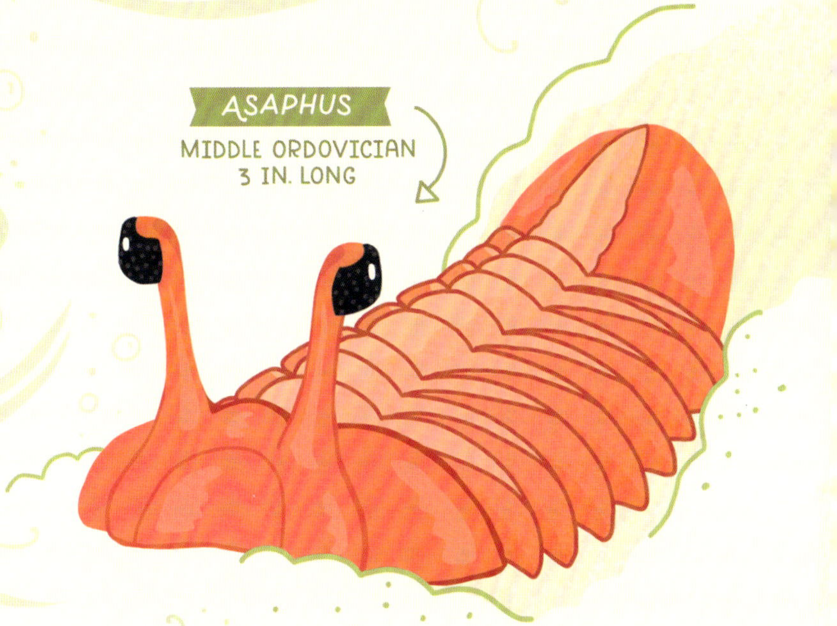

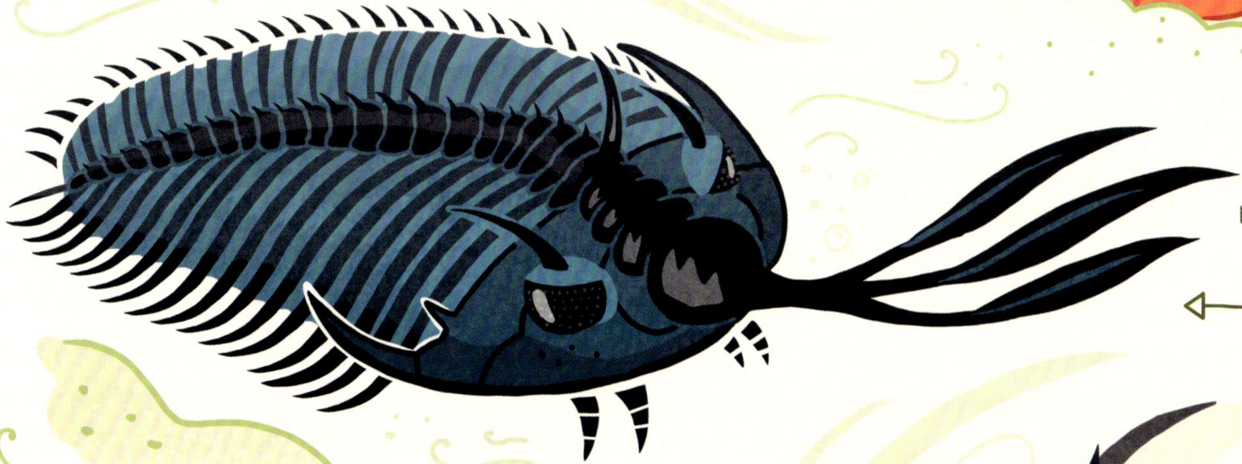

WALLISEROPS

EARLY TO MIDDLE DEVONIAN
3½ IN. LONG

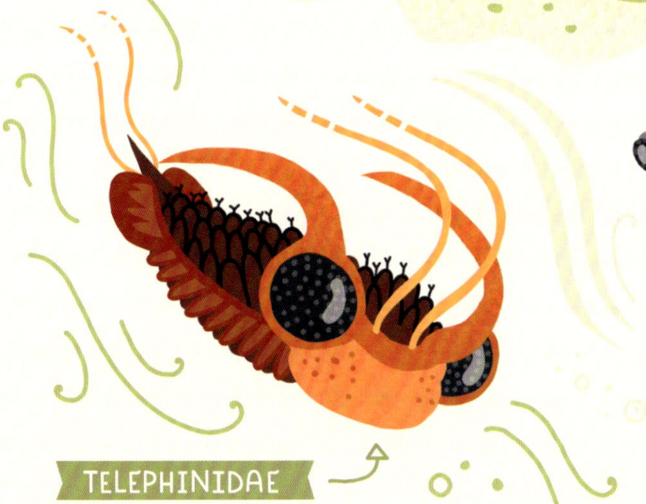

TELEPHINIDAE

EARLY TO LATE ORDOVICIAN
½ IN. LONG

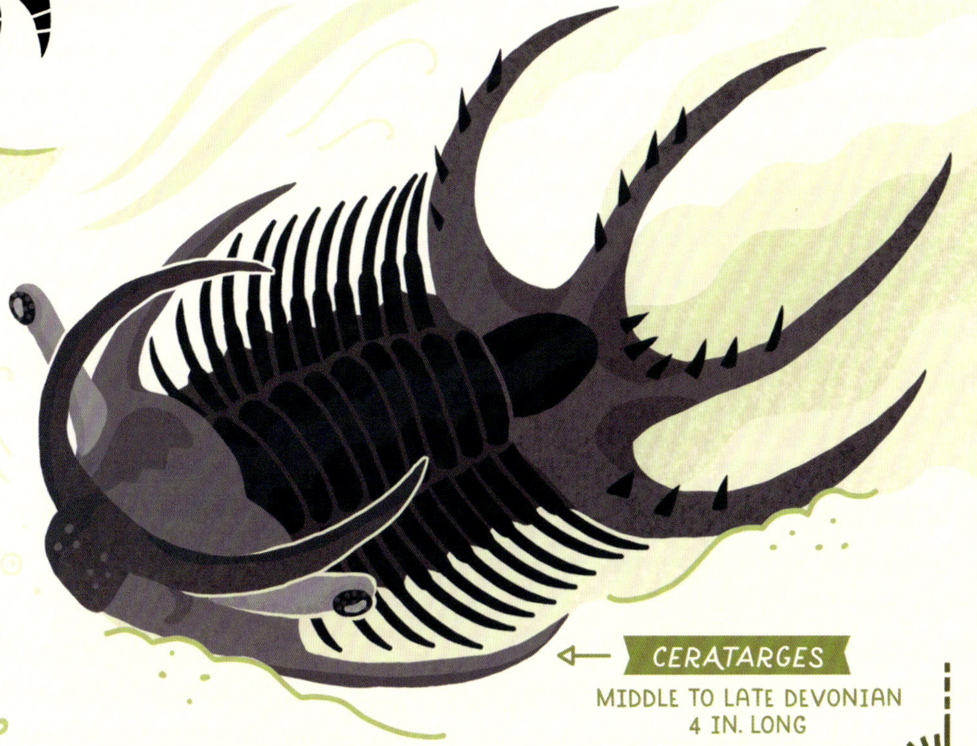

CERATARGES

MIDDLE TO LATE DEVONIAN
4 IN. LONG

THE ORDOVICIAN PERIOD

485 MILLION YEARS TO 443 MILLION YEARS AGO

CYRTOCERAS →

PANDERODUS →

IOCRINUS →

RHYNCHONELLIFORMEA

RED ALGAE

STARFISH →

Strange jawless fishes, giant tentacled cephalopods, and wiggling starfishes all lived among the new corals reefs of the Ordovician oceans. These animals evolved during the Great Ordovician Biodiversification Event. A new food web emerged, and at its base was photosynthesizing green algae, which, in turn, were eaten by microscopic primary consumers like plankton. This made up the base of a complex biome of animals and reefs. The earlier bottom-dwelling creepy-crawlies of the Cambrian were slowly replaced with an abundance of free-swimming animals.

Earth was a water world. The seafloor was raised by tectonic activity, which created vast underwater mountain ranges and raised sea levels. Almost the entirety of North America was underwater during this time. Evidence of this can be seen today in the many fossils of mollusks and crinoid tubes in limestone found in the eastern United States. In this environment of unstable sea levels, the first simple plants adapted to land, probably from surviving seasonal dry periods in coastal swamps. These fragile little plants covered the ground like modern liverworts and soon blanketed stones and gravel across the supercontinent of Gondwana.

Change is inevitable and sometimes catastrophic. The Late Ordovician mass extinction would end this period and be the first of Earth's five major mass extinction events. The extinction was sparked by primitive mossy land plants being "too successful." Newly evolved plants created so much oxygen in the atmosphere that it displaced warming greenhouse gases like carbon dioxide. This led the climate to change from a warm hothouse to an icehouse climate. Earth became covered in glaciers and global sea levels dropped by more than 500 feet. New cold waters and shallow coasts left ocean life frozen and stranded.

THE ORDOVICIAN PERIOD
LAND AND SEA

During the Ordovician Period, life flourished in an uninterrupted ocean named Panthalassa. Since there was only one supercontinent and no polar ice caps, the warm ocean currents were unimpeded. This meant sea animals could spread across the globe with little to interrupt their path. Today, many of the same fossil species from this time are found on opposite ends of the globe.

The usual reef resident animals, like sea urchins and feathery crinoids, appeared alongside ornately shelled mollusks. The Ordovician was a time when many unusual animals flourished, like *Pentecopterus*, a genus of sea scorpions that were the length of a person! In the midst of all this chaos, fishes were busy working on a new anatomy, with skeletons and jawless teeth. Vertebrates, animals with a backbone, were starting to be a big deal!

At the same time, plants were making evolutionary moves. Paleontologists believe that small moss-like plants first appeared in the ocean, then evolved to tolerate freshwater rivers and lakes. Finally, plants adapted to survive from rainwater on land by evolving a root system. These plants reproduced with spores so they could spread quickly. Their spores are found in the fossil record, allowing paleontologists to date the earliest plants on land. Although no purely terrestrial animals are known to have lived during the Ordovician, there are trace fossils of arthropods digging and wandering through the primitive soil crust. It would be millions of years before animals would truly inherit the land.

FUN FACTS:

The boundaries of the Ordovician Period were marked by feuding British scientists. Adam Sedgwick claimed the time span belonged to the Cambrian Period, while Roderick Murchison claimed it was part of the Silurian Period. The debate lasted for over a century.

Ordovician deposits are a source of fossil fuels. In 1859 Pennsylvania, the first oil well was dug from limestone dated to this period.

Two giant asteroids collided between Mars and Jupiter, causing the Ordovician sky to be filled with 100 times as many meteorites than are seen today. These L chondrite fragments continue to impact Earth.

The summit of Mount Everest was on the ocean floor during the Ordovician.

CONODONT JAW FOSSILS

STORIES OF DISCOVERY:

APATOKEPHALUS

FOULONIA

COLPOCORYPHE

Many of the best-preserved fossils of the Ordovician come from the Sahara Desert in Morocco. Since the 1980s, hundreds of trilobite species have been discovered under the sand dunes and in the Atlas Mountains. Digging in this area started when just a few trilobites were found by chance outside of the city of Casablanca by a French geologist during World War I. Later, copper and zinc miners would regularly stumble upon strange bug-looking fossils entombed in rocks, which they would sell as curiosities. Today, trilobite fossils are a large part of Morocco's economy. Specimens of Moroccan fossil preparers' work are found in museums and collections worldwide.

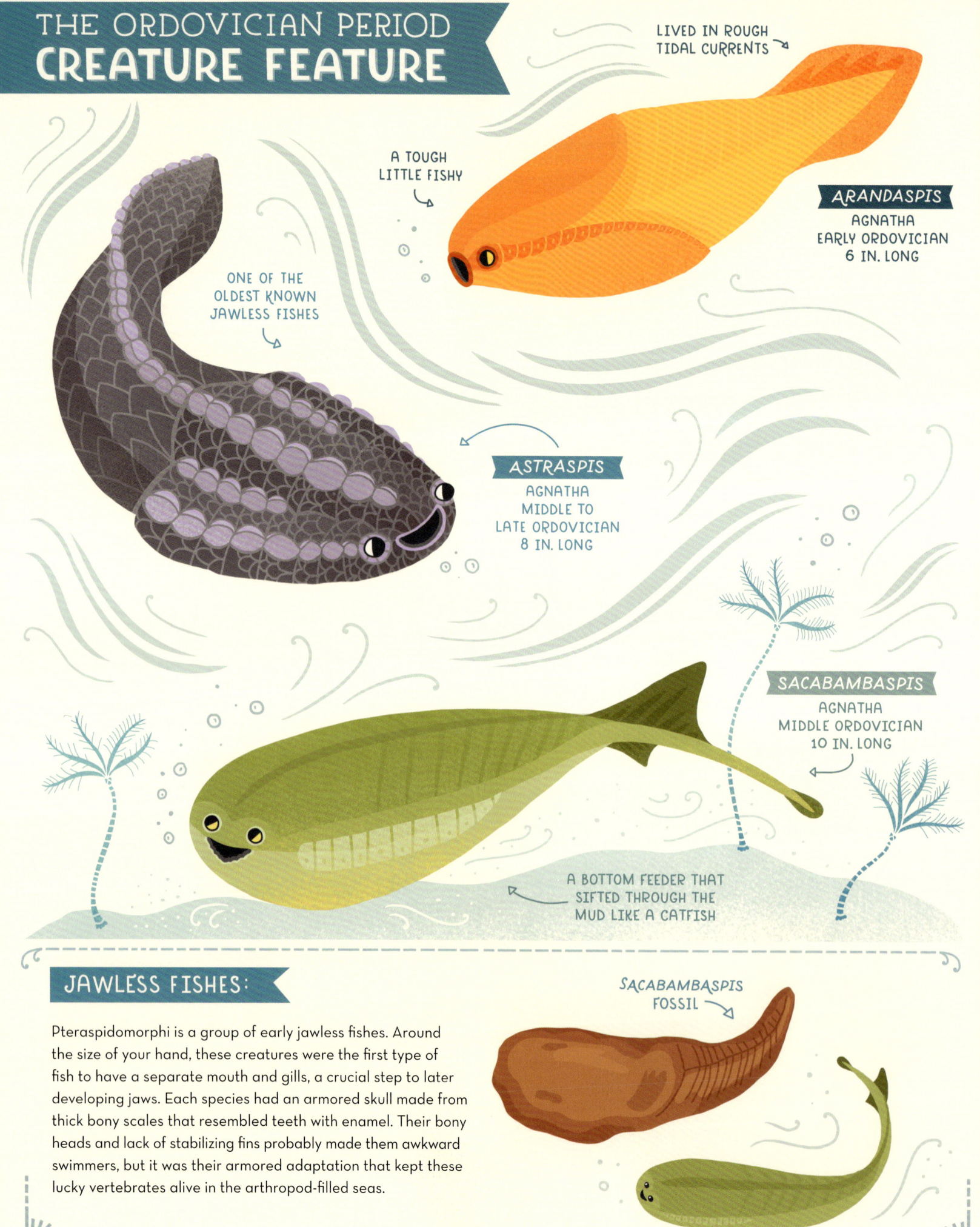

LIVED IN ROUGH TIDAL CURRENTS

A TOUGH LITTLE FISHY

ARANDASPIS
AGNATHA
EARLY ORDOVICIAN
6 IN. LONG

ONE OF THE OLDEST KNOWN JAWLESS FISHES

ASTRASPIS
AGNATHA
MIDDLE TO
LATE ORDOVICIAN
8 IN. LONG

SACABAMBASPIS
AGNATHA
MIDDLE ORDOVICIAN
10 IN. LONG

A BOTTOM FEEDER THAT SIFTED THROUGH THE MUD LIKE A CATFISH

JAWLESS FISHES:

Pteraspidomorphi is a group of early jawless fishes. Around the size of your hand, these creatures were the first type of fish to have a separate mouth and gills, a crucial step to later developing jaws. Each species had an armored skull made from thick bony scales that resembled teeth with enamel. Their bony heads and lack of stabilizing fins probably made them awkward swimmers, but it was their armored adaptation that kept these lucky vertebrates alive in the arthropod-filled seas.

SACABAMBASPIS FOSSIL

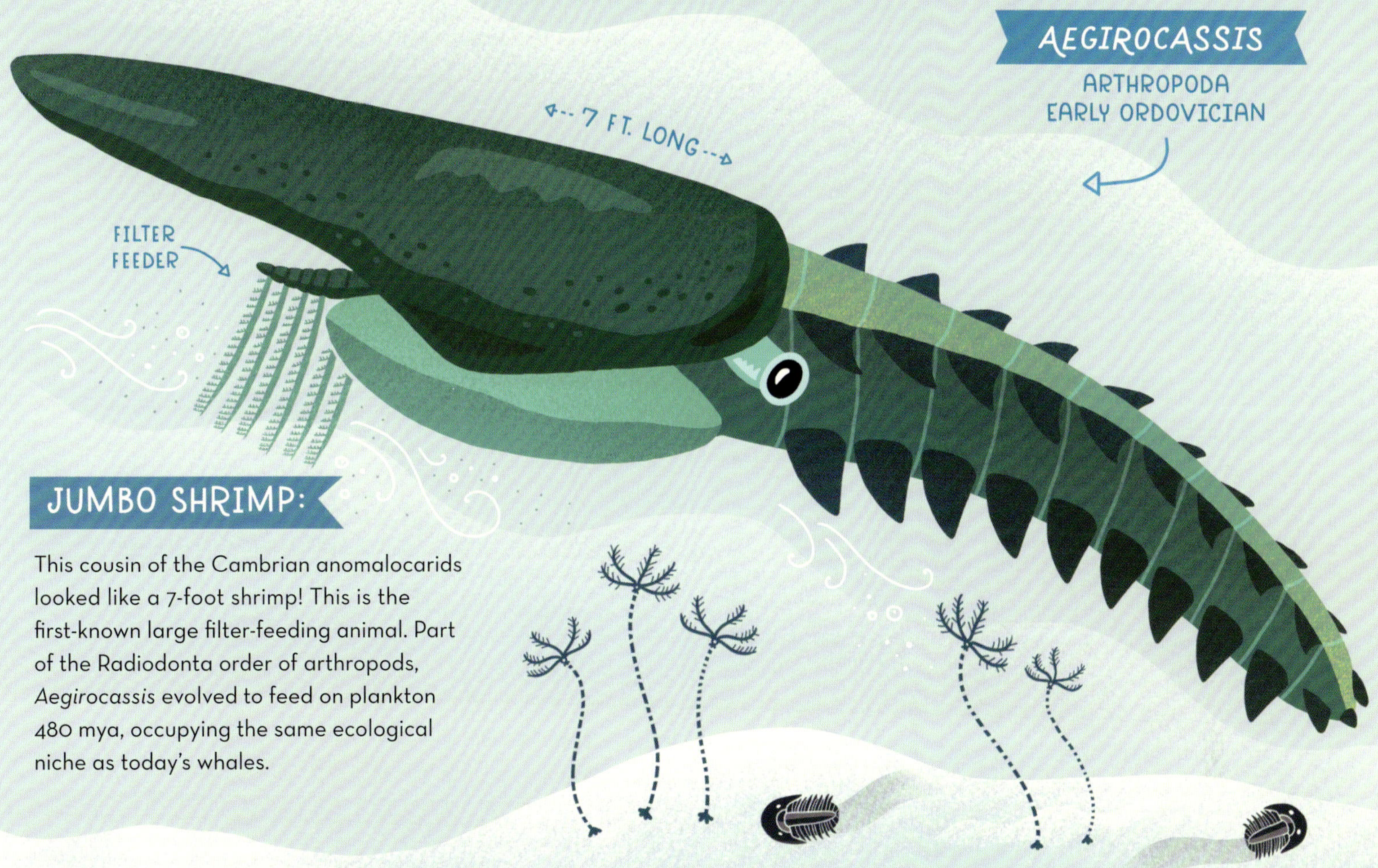

⟵-- 7 FT. LONG --⟶

FILTER
FEEDER

JUMBO SHRIMP:

This cousin of the Cambrian anomalocarids looked like a 7-foot shrimp! This is the first-known large filter-feeding animal. Part of the Radiodonta order of arthropods, *Aegirocassis* evolved to feed on plankton 480 mya, occupying the same ecological niche as today's whales.

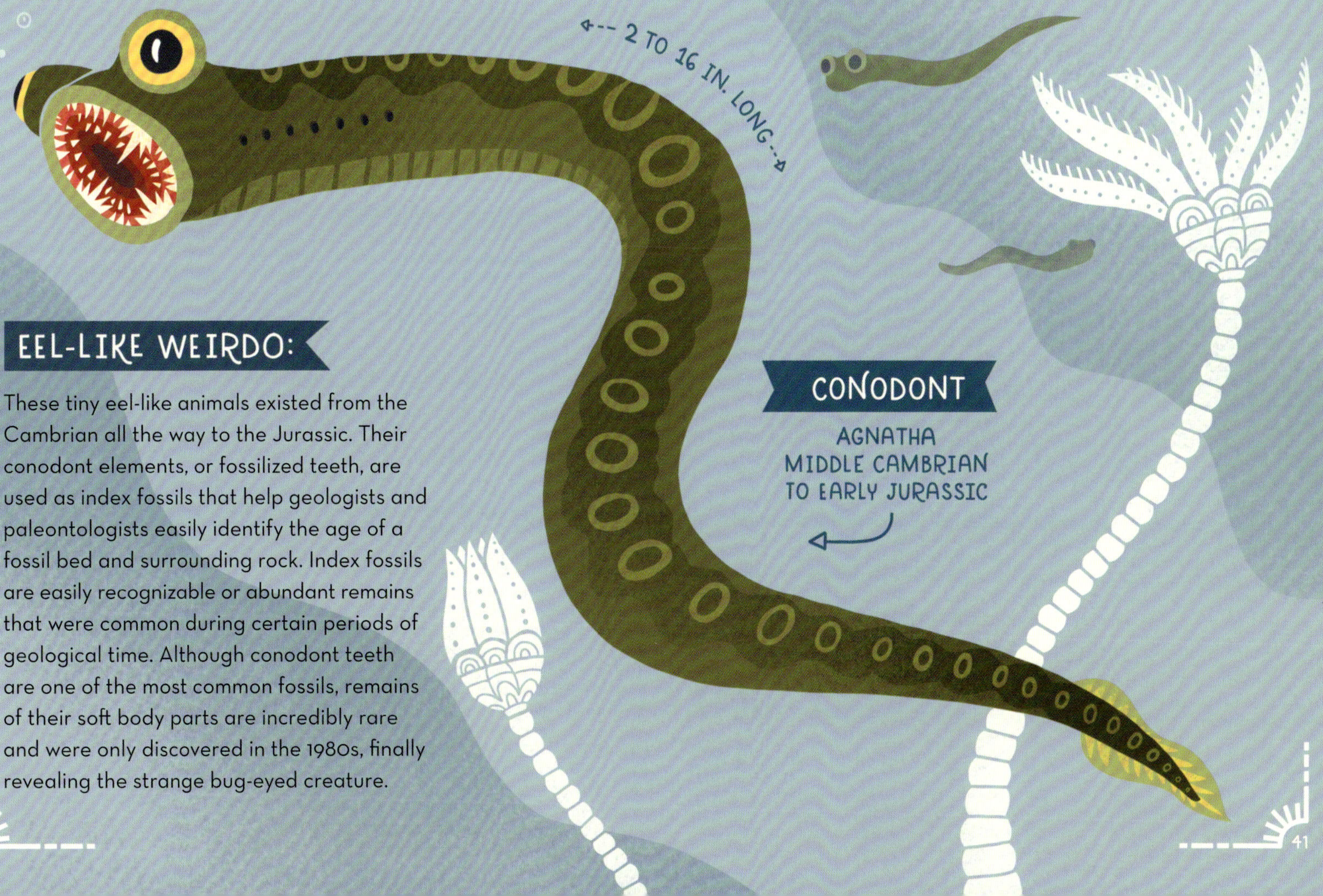

⟵-- 2 TO 16 IN. LONG --⟶

EEL-LIKE WEIRDO:

These tiny eel-like animals existed from the Cambrian all the way to the Jurassic. Their conodont elements, or fossilized teeth, are used as index fossils that help geologists and paleontologists easily identify the age of a fossil bed and surrounding rock. Index fossils are easily recognizable or abundant remains that were common during certain periods of geological time. Although conodont teeth are one of the most common fossils, remains of their soft body parts are incredibly rare and were only discovered in the 1980s, finally revealing the strange bug-eyed creature.

CONODONT

AGNATHA
MIDDLE CAMBRIAN
TO EARLY JURASSIC

THE SILURIAN
PERIOD

The Late Ordovician extinction left the oceans with an empty, dried-up seabed filled with bones and shells. An estimated 85 percent of all animal species were killed by the extreme cold. What came next during the Silurian Period was a relatively calm phase in Earth's history where the oceans heated back up. The ice caps melted, and Silurian oceans were transformed to shallow seas with giant coral reefs. It was in this warm and stable environment that in a "quick" span of 24 million years, life made some significant changes.

During the Silurian, the first small vascular plants with stems appeared on land, along with the first-known terrestrial animals. These animals were not the "fish with feet" often depicted in pop culture. The accomplishment of being the first land-dweller belongs to a millipede-like arthropod that crawled on dozens of legs. Many of the firsts in evolution belong to hard-shelled invertebrates. The first animal to take a big gulp of fresh air while sunning itself by the beach was definitely a large bug.

At the same time, fishes were evolving beyond googly-eyed, bottom-feeding mud vacuums. Silurian fishes were the first vertebrates with jaws that could open, close, and bite! A group called acanthodians were active predators with sharp bony jaws that sped through the water. These animals were the ancestors of modern sharks and were the size of a goldfish.

Despite having new abilities, vertebrates had not yet fought to the top of the food chain. That gruesome throne still belonged to nautiloids and a terrifying order of giant sea scorpions called Eurypterida. For the moment, spineless invertebrates would still rule the world.

TUJIAASPIS
VIVIDUS

XIUSHANOSTEUS
MIRABILIS

SHENACANTHUS
VERMIFORMIS

2 IN. TALL

SPORES

COOKSONIA

PALAEOTARBUS JERAMI

PNEUMODESMUS NEWMANI

TORTILICAULIS

COWIELEPIS

POLEUMITA

THE SILURIAN PERIOD
LAND AND SEA

Dating as far back as the Cambrian Period, there has been evidence of fossilized animal tracks showing aquatic arthropods briefly leaving the water to scurry around on the beach. But it was during the Silurian Period that animals began to live full-time on dry land. The earliest-known terrestrial animal was a small myriapod called *Pneumodesmus* that looked a lot like a modern millipede. It likely munched on plant litter on the beaches of what is now Scotland. *Pneumodesmus* had spiracles, small holes on its body for breathing air into its body. These holes are found today on insects. Scientists take the presence of these spiracles on the fossilized *Pneumodesmus* as definitive proof that it lived a dry existence, since aquatic arthropods lack spiracles. This is a big step in evolution!

Bacteria of the Silurian Period may not have been able to quickly break down plant debris, which left an abundance of decaying plant matter for new land animals to eat. And there were a lot of plants! The first vascular plant, *Cooksonia*, had spread to coastal areas worldwide. Without any leaves or flowers, the 2-inch-tall *Cooksonia* could still perform photosynthesis and carried nutrients and water through its stem. These simple plants made up the base of the new terrestrial food chain. While myriapods munched on plants, they were hunted by fierce arachnids! By the end of the Silurian, a land-based ecosystem had fully formed around coastal wetlands.

FUN FACTS:

Trigonotarbida, ancestors of spiders, lived in swamps and probably hunted early myriapods.

Plants like *Cooksonia* flourished so much that they fueled the first wildfire, which paleontologists have dated to 430 mya. This evidence proves that there was enough oxygen in the atmosphere to support a large fire.

The first-known true scorpion, *Palaeophonus* (428 mya to 314 mya), was likely semi-aquatic. Its name means "ancient killer" in Greek.

STORIES OF DISCOVERY:

FISH MODEL

TONS OF TINY FISH FOSSILS FOUND TOGETHER

Settled 3,800 feet high, in the foggy mountains above the city of Chongqing in southwestern China, is a steep road with forty-five hairpin turns that leads to the mountain village of Chuanhegai. This impressive road was built in 2015. Its construction required carving out bedrock that ended up exposing miles of difficult-to-access Silurian-aged stone. Paleontologists Min Zhu and Qiang Li had suspected the area could hold fossils. They were pleasantly surprised when one of the steep corners of the road contained a perfectly preserved armored fish, sticking right out of the side of the cliff! The area was searched further in 2020, revealing several species of early jawed fishes at the highest grade of fossil preservation. This discovery pushed back the date of the first-known jawed vertebrates by 14 million years.

··THE SILURIAN PERIOD··
CREATURE FEATURE

CARCINOSOMA
ARTHROPODA
EARLY TO LATE SILURIAN
7 FT. LONG

ITS NAME MEANS "CRAB BODY."

EURYPTERUS
ARTHROPODA
MIDDLE TO LATE
SILURIAN
8 IN. LONG

FOSSIL FIRST DISCOVERED IN 1818 IN THE BERTIE FORMATION IN NEW YORK

SHARP TAIL SPINE WAS USED FOR DEFENSE AND FOR HUNTING.

MIXOPTERUS
ARTHROPODA
LATE SILURIAN
30 IN. LONG

SLIMONIA
ARTHROPODA
MIDDLE TO LATE SILURIAN
3 FT. LONG

LIKELY A POOR SWIMMER THAT CRAWLED ALONG THE OCEAN FLOOR

EURYPTERIDS, THE GIANT SCORPIONS:

Man-sized scorpions are the thing of nightmares, and 430 mya the seas and rivers were full of them. The largest arthropods to have ever lived were an order called Eurypterida. Although they resemble scorpions, they are only distantly related and did not often venture onto dry land—probably because of their weight. Large eurypterids were most likely the apex predator during the Silurian and Early Devonian Periods, using their giant claws to capture whatever unlucky animal came near.

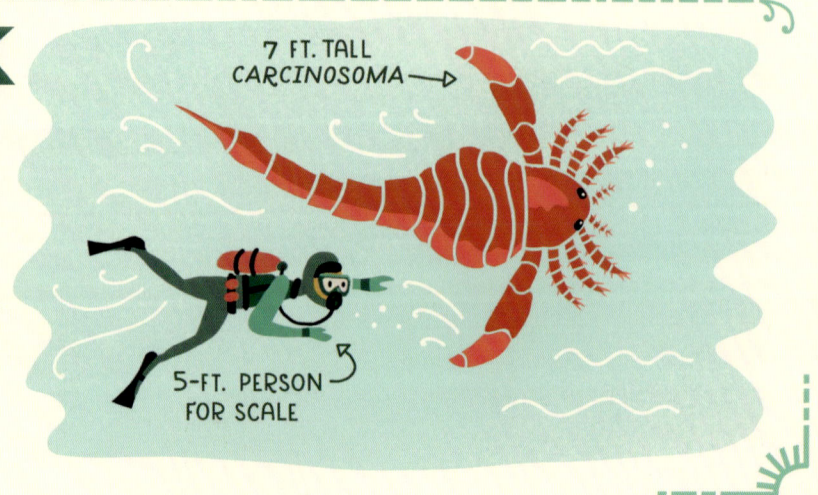

7 FT. TALL CARCINOSOMA →

5-FT. PERSON FOR SCALE

GUIYU ONEIROS
OSTEICHTHYES
LATE SILURIAN
1 FT. LONG ➜

ONE OF THE EARLIEST-
KNOWN BONY FISHES,
WHOSE SKELETONS
WERE MADE FROM
BONE INSTEAD OF
CARTILAGE

PSAROLEPIS
OSTEICHTHYES
LATE SILURIAN TO
EARLY DEVONIAN
4 IN. LONG

QIANODUS
CHONDRICHTHYES
EARLY SILURIAN

MAY HAVE
BEEN A FEW
INCHES LONG

EARLY JAWED FISHES:

The earliest-known teeth from a vertebrate belonged
to a mysterious fish from 439 mya. Since *Qianodus* likely
had a skeleton made from cartilage, its body was not
preserved in fossils. However, the fish's many tooth whorls
were fossilized and resemble the dental growth patterns
of shark ancestors, the acanthodians.

Jaws were a game changer. Fishes with jaws could
obviously bite and chew food, but jaws could also serve
as a shovel for digging burrows and unearthing food.
With jaws, vertebrates had the ability to actively modify
their environment to better suit their needs.

ONE OF THE
OLDEST-KNOWN
VERTEBRATES
WITH JAWS

FOUND IN
CHINA

THE DEVONIAN PERIOD

419 MILLION YEARS TO 359 MILLION YEARS AGO

Calling the Devonian Period the age of the fishes is an understatement. During this time, much of Earth's continents were covered by warm and shallow seas. It's thought that corals covered over 3 million square miles, ten times the number of reefs today. In a diverse network of corals, the tiny fishes of the previous period grew a lot larger. Taking cues from their arthropod competitors, vertebrates evolved tough armored bodies to survive. The major fish group of this time was the placoderms, which had bony skulls and shearing jaws. Larger placoderm predators were so vicious that they drove many animals out of marine environments into inland rivers, shallow swamps, and eventually dry land!

By the Middle Devonian, the first trees reached skyward. Out of competition for sunlight, plants that were packed tightly across the coastal plains had to evolve structures to maintain height. Deep root systems and sturdy wood tissue allowed the first trees to tower over the landscape.

These flourishing early land-based ecosystems would be put to the test by the Late Devonian mass extinction event. The cause is still a mystery, but theories include a meteor impact, volcanic activity, a nearby star supernova, or a combination of all these. Nevertheless, a few spunky survivors from this time would go on to be the ancestors of tetrapods, a group made up of all land-living vertebrates, including frogs, lizards, dinosaurs, birds, people, and more!

ANEUROPHYTALEAN RHIZOMES

ATTERCOPUS

DRACOCHELA

DREPANOPHYCUS

CHEIROLEPIS

MIGUASHAIA

BRACHIOPOD

THE DEVONIAN PERIOD
LAND AND SEA

Of all the living things in Earth's history, we can thank a single species of tree for making dry land much more habitable for animals. *Archaeopteris* is the first-ever wooded tree with leaves, and it wouldn't look out of place today. These trees had massive root systems that broke down rocks, releasing minerals that enriched the soil. The tangled roots also prevented erosion. Animals began to have stable footing on dry land, without worrying about constant mudslides! In addition, dead leaves, twigs, and fallen trunks created animal habitats and kickstarted new ecosystems. Forests made up of only *Archaeopteris* spread worldwide—even into the Arctic Circle. As they grew, they terraformed the landscape into a more hospitable place, changing Earth's surface forever.

It was in swamps among *Archaeopteris* trees that the first tetrapods left their watery homes. Driven by danger, lobe-finned fishes sought out oxygen-poor shallows where their predators couldn't survive. These animals breathed with gills like any other fish, but above the water's surface they could breathe with a small pair of lungs. It was an advantage that, paired with muscular front fins originally used to crawl among coral, would allow them to go on excursions on land searching for a different pond to call home or a tasty arthropod snack. The combination of lungs and limbs is a perfect example of two unrelated adaptations that, when put together by chance, can change everything. This was the greatest evolutionary combination since eyeballs and mouths.

FUN FACTS:

Today's Australian lungfish is a living fossil that has gills and lungs. Humans share a common ancestor with lungfishes that lived 400 mya.

ASK IF YOUR LOCAL AQUARIUM HAS A LUNGFISH!

SPLASH

Ferns evolved seeds in the Late Devonian. Seeds are tougher and can spread farther than spores, which dry out easily.

Arachnids called harvestmen (also known as daddy long-legs) have been crawling around for at least 400 million years.

HAVING LONG LEGS AND A TINY HEAD WORKS FOR ME!

WHERE DID ALL THE OXYGEN GO?

?

During the mysterious Late Devonian extinction event, the oxygen in the atmosphere may have dropped below 13 percent. A clue is that no wildfires are recorded around 380 mya.

STORIES OF DISCOVERY:

TIKTAALIK

9 TO 14 FT. LONG

TIKTAALIK FOSSIL →

Many fossils of salamander-like animals have been discovered from the Late Devonian, but there was a large gap between the fishes and the land crawlers. For over a century, there was a missing link in the fossil history of tetrapodomorphs (fishes with limbs). Many paleontologists predicted a transitional animal would eventually be found. In 2004, it finally happened—they discovered *Tiktaalik*, a fish with very tetrapod-like features! In the remote arctic of Canada, a *Tiktaalik* skull was found sticking out of the side of a cliff by paleontologists. This fossil formation on Ellesmere Island was near the equator 375 mya. *Tiktaalik* would have swum around tropical streams and probably behaved like a crocodile snatching prey from the water's edge. The name *Tiktaalik* comes from the Inuktitut word for "large freshwater fish."

THE DEVONIAN PERIOD
CREATURE FEATURE

DUNKLEOSTEUS TERRELLI

PLACODERMI
LATE DEVONIAN

<-- 20 FT. LONG -->

JAWS WERE RAZOR-SHARP FOR SLICING PREY.

IT HAD HEAVY ARMORED BONY PLATES.

SELF-SHARPENING BONES: WHEN THE JAWS RUBBED TOGETHER, THE KNIFE-LIKE UPPER JAW WAS SHARPENED.

REVENGE OF THE FISH:

Dunkleosteus terrelli was the "big bad" of the Devonian ocean. With a huge, shearing bite, this monstrous fish could crush anything that fit in its jaw. Using mechanical models, paleobiologists have estimated *Dunkleosteus* could open and close its jaw in 50 milliseconds, faster than the blink of an eye. In one quick, powerful movement it could suck prey right into its mouth, similar to how modern bass hunt. The adult *Dunkleosteus* was the first vertebrate apex predator, and it fed on former apex predators like the eurypterids (sea scorpions) and giant squids. The adults even ate other *Dunkleosteus*—evidence of this was left as battle scars on their fossilized bones. There is some debate about the actual size of the fish, since the only fossilized remains are of the armored skull. Some paleontologists believe *Dunkleosteus* were short and stubby like a bulldog, while others think they might have been long like giant sharks.

YUM!

CRUNCH

SHORT OR LONG? ? ? ?

TRANSITIONAL FISH
BETWEEN THOSE WITH
FINS AND LIMBS

ICHTHYOSTEGA
SARCOPTERYGII
LATE DEVONIAN
3 FT. LONG

FLOP

ONE OF THE EARLIEST ANIMALS TO
ADAPT LIMBS FOR NON-SWIMMING,
ITS FEET HAD 7 TOES♥

PANDERICHTHYS
SARCOPTERYGII
LATE DEVONIAN
6 FT. LONG

PARMASTEGA
SARCOPTERYGII
LATE DEVONIAN
4 FT. LONG

MOST LIKELY LIVED AT THE
WATER'S SURFACE, BASED ON
ITS CROCODILE-LIKE EYEBALLS

LACKED GILLS
AS AN ADULT

TULERPETON
SARCOPTERYGII
LATE DEVONIAN
3 FT. LONG

FROM SWIMMING TO WALKING:

Fishes with legs were a common sight in the Middle to Late Devonian. This group of animals, called tetrapodomorphs, had flipped, flopped, and crawled across the world's coasts and rivers to the point where they are found in fossil deposits worldwide. These animals faced an extremely harsh environment during the Late Devonian extinction event. Their ability to breathe air with lungs and escape aquatic predators on land ensured that at least one species of tetrapodomorph survived to become the ancestor of all land vertebrates.

THE CARBONIFEROUS PERIOD

359 MILLION YEARS TO 299 MILLION YEARS AGO

The Carboniferous Earth was a hazy world of endless swamps and rainforests. Orange skies were filled with the smoke of perpetually burning forest fires. Flying insects the size of hawks darted about, while dog-sized amphibians howled. Things got weird during this period of Earth history, and we can thank a microbial hiccup for setting the mood.

Trees release oxygen and absorb carbon dioxide from the air, and trees store this carbon as they grow. Microbial decomposers from the Carboniferous like bacteria and fungi had trouble breaking down the newly evolved wood cellulose. Tree trunks and branches that fell to the forest floor just piled up instead of returning to the food web. As carbon dioxide became trapped in dead trees, the atmospheric oxygen content rose to a staggering 35 percent! Animals adapted to much higher oxygen levels. Arthropods grew to the largest sizes of all time, so their simple respiratory systems could function in the thick air. The 8-foot-long *Arthropleura* millipede was the largest terrestrial invertebrate ever, wandering around munching on ferns without a care in the world.

While invertebrates were living large, terrestrial vertebrates divided into two lineages: the amphibians and the amniotes. Amphibians would retain some of the fish-like ways of their ancestors. They laid eggs in water and had a life cycle based on metamorphosis. Meanwhile, amniotes could live far from a water source, could lay eggs with shells that retained moisture on dry land, and had scaly skin. Paleontologists haven't discovered the exact fossil yet, but a small lizard-shaped amniote from the Middle Carboniferous is the common ancestor of all reptiles, birds, and mammals.

ARTHROPLEURA

OPHIDERPETON

WESTLOTHIANA

THE CARBONIFEROUS PERIOD
LAND AND SEA

Around 305 mya, the continent-spanning rainforests had shrunk due to a minor extinction event called the Carboniferous Rainforest Collapse. The forests dried out and only patches of swampland remained. This drier climate was no longer the amphibian-friendly paradise of the Early Carboniferous. Instead, it favored animals that could withstand an arid climate and set in motion the diversification of amniotes.

Amniotes divided into two main groups: the synapsids and the early reptiles. At first, the difference between synapsids and reptiles was small: just the number of jaw-muscle holes (temporal fenestrae) in their skull. Synapsids were the first to evolve the ability to self-regulate their body temperature, giving them a competitive edge. On a cold foggy morning, a synapsid predator like *Ophiacodon* would have been up and hunting before groggy amphibians and reptiles, who were waiting for the sun to wake their metabolism. These early synapsids are the far-off distant ancestor of another group of warm-blooded animals—the mammals!

During the Late Carboniferous, insects took to the sky and became Earth's first flying animals! Insects had modified exoskeleton plates attached to their legs that, over time, migrated to the top of their bodies to form transparent wings. Early flying insects, like *Meganeura*, looked like giant dragonflies and were active predators. Other insects that looked like big cockroaches evolved foldable wings that could be tucked away for easier movement on the ground. Flying was useful for dodging attacks from the hungry reptiles that lived along the swamps.

FUN FACTS:

At some point in the Early Carboniferous, tetrapod evolution settled on five digits for each foot. It's why humans only have five fingers per hand today.

HYLONOMUS EITHER LIVED INSIDE THE LYCOPODS OR WERE TRAPPED INSIDE!

IS IT MY HOUSE OR MY TOMB?!

The earliest-known reptile is *Hylonomus* (312 mya). Its fossils are only found inside the stumps of fallen lycopods.

Meganeura was a giant insect with a wingspan over 2 feet. It hunted in the sky and was a flying ace!

RUN AWAY.

STORIES OF DISCOVERY:

300 MYA

COMPACTED DEAD PLANTS TURN INTO PEAT.

100 MYA

TIME AND PRESSURE

PEAT TURNS INTO LIGNITE.

TODAY

TIME AND PRESSURE

LIGNITE TURNS INTO COAL.

Ninety percent of Earth's coal deposits date back to the Carboniferous and Permian Periods. Microbes from this time could not decompose wood. Over time, heat and pressure from the earth turned preserved forest debris into the coal beds that are found worldwide. Coal is a highly combustible fossil fuel that has been used to smelt metals for more than 5,000 years. In ancient Rome and China, people tapped into exposed coal outcroppings for their furnaces. Starting in the 18th century, during the Industrial Revolution in England, coal was used to super-heat water to power steam engines for large factories, trains, and ships.

When coal is burned, it combines with the oxygen in the atmosphere to create carbon dioxide. According to the Environmental Protection Agency, for each pound of coal burned, 2.07 pounds of carbon dioxide is created. Today, burned coal makes up 25 percent of modern energy consumption. Its pollution is a large contributor to current global warming. Scientists hypothesize that burning all of Earth's coal deposits could return carbon dioxide levels to a hot climate similar to the age of the dinosaurs.

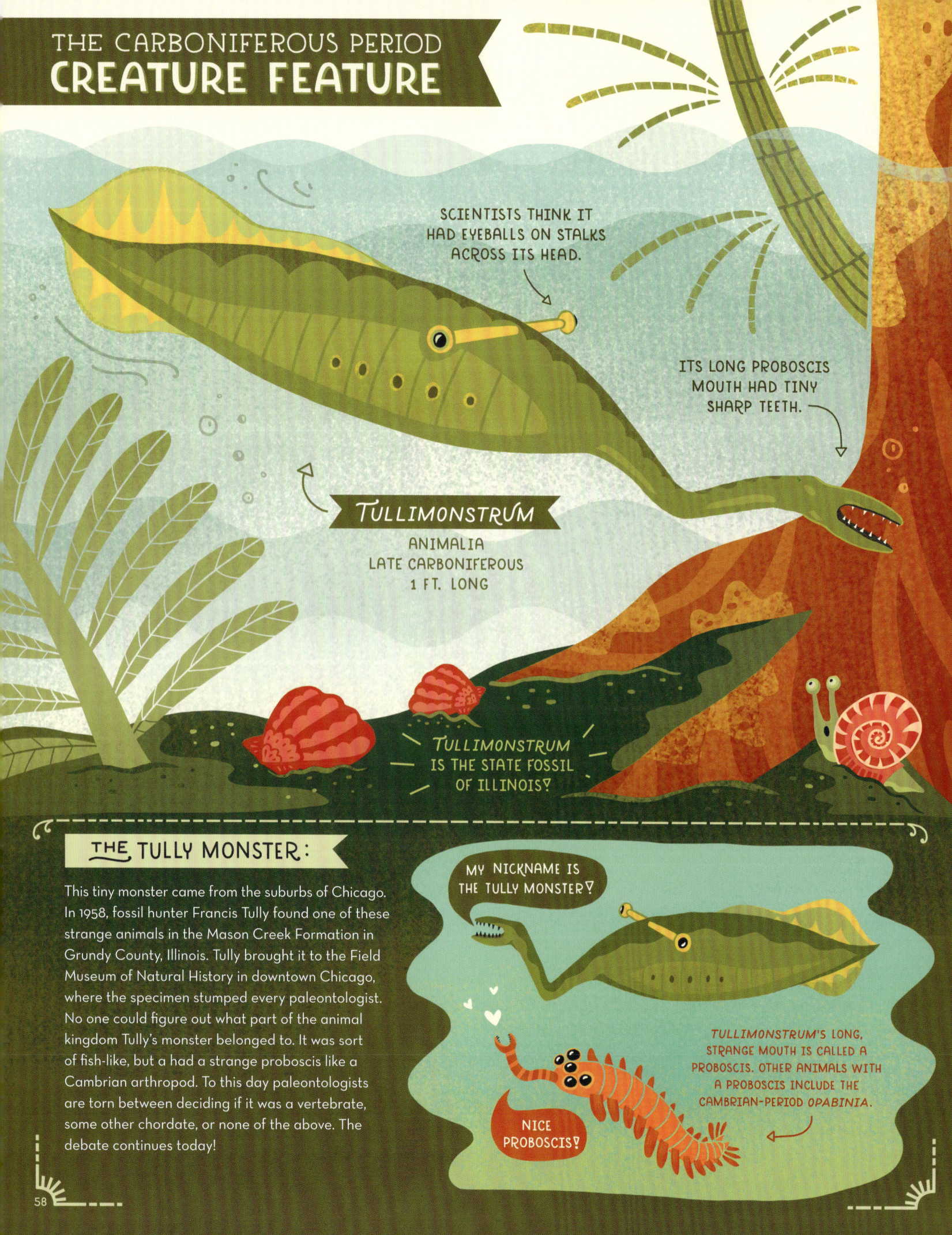

SCIENTISTS THINK IT HAD EYEBALLS ON STALKS ACROSS ITS HEAD.

ITS LONG PROBOSCIS MOUTH HAD TINY SHARP TEETH.

TULLIMONSTRUM

ANIMALIA
LATE CARBONIFEROUS
1 FT. LONG

TULLIMONSTRUM IS THE STATE FOSSIL OF ILLINOIS!

THE TULLY MONSTER:

This tiny monster came from the suburbs of Chicago. In 1958, fossil hunter Francis Tully found one of these strange animals in the Mason Creek Formation in Grundy County, Illinois. Tully brought it to the Field Museum of Natural History in downtown Chicago, where the specimen stumped every paleontologist. No one could figure out what part of the animal kingdom Tully's monster belonged to. It was sort of fish-like, but a had a strange proboscis like a Cambrian arthropod. To this day paleontologists are torn between deciding if it was a vertebrate, some other chordate, or none of the above. The debate continues today!

MY NICKNAME IS THE TULLY MONSTER!

NICE PROBOSCIS!

TULLIMONSTRUM'S LONG, STRANGE MOUTH IS CALLED A PROBOSCIS. OTHER ANIMALS WITH A PROBOSCIS INCLUDE THE CAMBRIAN-PERIOD OPABINIA.

JUVENILES WERE
4 TO 6 IN. LONG?

CHONDRICHTHYES
LATE CARBONIFEROUS
10 FT. LONG

ITS TINY FEET
WERE USELESS
ON LAND.

CRASSIGYRINUS

SARCOPTERYGII
MIDDLE CARBONIFEROUS
9 TO 13 FT. LONG

ADULTS LIVED IN FRESH WATER,
AND YOUNG LIVED IN SALT WATER.

ANVIL-SHAPED
DORSAL FINS WERE
ONLY FOUND IN MALES.

FRESHWATER
PREDATOR

STETHACANTHUS

HOLOCEPHALI
LATE DEVONIAN TO
LATE CARBONIFEROUS
5 TO 9 FT. LONG

WHORLED
TEETH SLICED
THROUGH PREY.

EDESTUS

HOLOCEPHALI
LATE CARBONIFEROUS
22 FT. LONG

A PREDATOR THE SIZE OF
A GREAT WHITE SHARK

PREDATORS IN THE WATER:

Although life was getting exciting on land during the
Carboniferous Period, there was still a lot of action
happening underwater. Fishes with strangely shaped
teeth and jaws hunted in both the salty ocean and in
freshwater rivers. Fossils have been found showing
off these odd-looking predators.

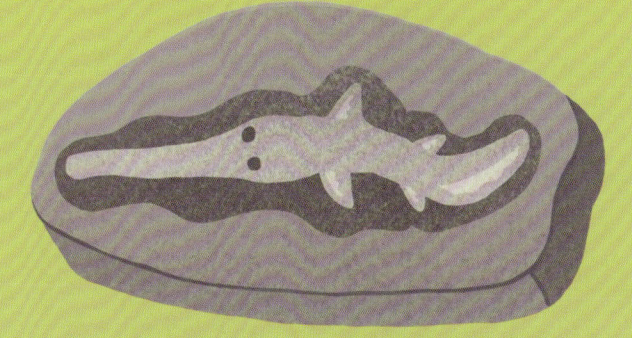

JUVENILE
BANDRINGA
SHARK FOSSIL

EDAPHOSAURUS→

LABIDOSAURIKOS→

DIADECTES→

SECODONTOSAURUS→

VARANOSAURUS→

←LABIDOSAURUS

DIPLOCAULUS→

THE PERMIAN PERIOD

299 MILLION YEARS TO 252 MILLION YEARS AGO

During the Permian Period, the world came together. Not in a "hold hands and sing for world peace" kind of way, but instead landmasses were united, literally, as one gigantic supercontinent called Pangea. Tectonic plates slowly smashed together, and Pangea fully assembled around 299 mya as the largest landmass to ever exist. It was accompanied by an uninterrupted global ocean called Panthalassa.

The sun baked down on the center of Pangea, creating giant deserts framed by costal swamplands and elevated montane forests. Over time, many amphibians could not survive the new arid terrain, but reptiles thrived and diversified. These reptiles are the ancient ancestors to familiar animal groups like dinosaurs, crocodiles, lizards, and birds. Another group that became widespread at this time were synapsids. While early synapsids like *Edaphosaurus* are often mistaken as the ancestors of dinosaurs, they are in fact the long-distant relative to mammals.

The Permian Period ended with the "Great Dying," which was the most devastating mass extinction in all of Earth's history. Also known as the Permian–Triassic mass extinction event, most scientists believe it was triggered by volcanic activity in what is now the Siberian Traps. The release of greenhouse gasses like methane and carbon dioxide spewed out from cracks in Earth's crust, creating global warming. It was a slow-moving apocalypse, but only a snap of the fingers relative to geological time.

GRIFFENFLY

DIMETRODON

CAPTORHINUS

XENACANTHUS

GNATHORHIZA

GLOSSOPTERIS

STYRACOCEPHALUS

MOSCHOPS

BRADYSAURUS

GORGONOPS

LYCOSUCHUS

ROBERTIA

EUNOTOSAURUS

THE PERMIAN PERIOD
LAND AND SEA

The true stars of the Permian were the synapsids! These animals used to be described as mammal-like reptiles, but are more accurately called stem mammals. In the Early Permian Period, synapsids still looked extremely reptilian. As Pangea's climate changed to dry and arid, the synapsids evolved to have more mammal-like traits, including a more upright stance and complex teeth.

By the Middle Permian, synapsids like the ferocious saber-toothed *Gorgonops*, which looked like a combination of a lizard and wolf, roamed the cold steppes of what is now South Africa. Meanwhile, the crack of skulls could be heard in the distance as plant-eating *Moschops* slammed their hippo-sized bodies together as they headbutted for dominance. This advanced group of synapsids found during the Middle to Late Permian were called therapsids.

The climate had significantly warmed by the Late Permian due to volcanic eruptions, causing a slow die-off of many species. During the Permian–Triassic mass extinction event, the oceans acidified, oxygen levels decreased dramatically, ecosystems collapsed, and about 90 percent of all animal species went extinct. Even the trilobites, a group of arthropods that survived several mass extinctions and existed for 270 million years, were wiped out. The entire Paleozoic Era came to an end, and it would take millions of years for Earth's ecosystems to bounce back.

FUN FACTS:

ERYOPS

The Early Permian had amphibians like the small *Diplocaulus* and larger *Eryops*, which had a giant toothed frog-like mouth.

GLIDED LIKE A MODERN FLYING SQUIRREL

FOSSIL DISCOVERED IN GERMANY

One of the oldest-known gliding vertebrates was *Weigeltisaurus jaekeli*, a reptile that lived 255 mya.

WIDE RIBS ACTED AS A PROTO-SHELL.

Eunotosaurus africanus was an ancestor to modern turtles. Its wide ribs were a proto-shell.

STORIES OF DISCOVERY:

THE FIRST *MESOSAURUS* FOSSIL WAS FOUND IN 1830 IN THE CAPE OF SOUTH AFRICA.

IT'S RUMORED THAT IT WAS USED AS A POT LID.

AFRICA

SOUTH AMERICA

MESOSAURUS FOSSILS FOUND HERE →

For 100 million years, Earth had one supercontinent called Pangea. Key evidence of its existence can be seen in matching rock formations on opposite sides of the globe and the distribution of Permian and Triassic fossils. One major clue was the bones of a small, crocodile-like reptile called *Mesosaurus*. It lived during the Early Permian in the freshwater coastal shallows, where it caught fishes in its needle-toothed mouth. This 3-foot-long aquatic animal had lungs, not gills, so it needed to surface often for air. Multiple matching *Mesosaurus* fossils have been found on both the tip of South America and in Africa. Crossing the modern Atlantic Ocean would have been impossible for the small *Mesosaurus*, so for this to make any sense, the continents must have been connected during the Permian! Just look at a map and you can see how South America and Africa fit together like puzzle pieces. By understanding the behavior of one small extinct creature, we get clues about prehistoric geography!

···THE PERMIAN PERIOD··· CREATURE FEATURE

THE SMALLEST-KNOWN MEMBER OF THE *DIMETRODON* GROUP WAS ONLY 2 FT. LONG.

DIMETRODON ANGELENSIS

PELYCOSAUR SYNAPSID
EARLY PERMIAN

DIMETRODON MEANS "TWO MEASURES OF TOOTH." IT HAD CANINE FANGS IN ITS UPPER JAW AND SHORTER TEETH IN BACK, LIKE A DOG.

DIMETRODON TEUTONIS

◁--15 FT. LONG --▷

A FRILLED MYSTERY:

Synapsids are considered some of the first land-roaming megafauna (giant animals). None was fiercer and more feared than a genus of animals called *Dimetrodon*. One of the many synapsids with sail backs, *Dimetrodon* is considered the apex predator of the Early Permian Period. *Dimetrodon angelensis*, one of the largest-known species in this genus, stalked swampy wetlands of coastal Pangea to devour its prey.

The impressive sail found on *Dimetrodon* puzzled paleologists! At first, the sail was thought to regulate body temperature. This notion changed after paleologists compared the sail on multiple fossils of *Dimetrodon* at different ages and species big and small. It's now hypothesized the giant sail had a more social function and was most likely used to attract mates, boast strength, and scare off rivals.

ELONGATED SPINE BONES FORM A SAIL.

ESTEMMENOSUCHUS
THERAPSID SYNAPSID
MIDDLE PERMIAN
14 FT. LONG

NAME MEANS
"CROWNED CROCODILE"
IN GREEK.

LYSTROSAURUS MURRAYI
THERAPSID SYNAPSID
LATE PERMIAN TO EARLY TRIASSIC
2 TO 8 FT. LONG

IT SURVIVED
THE PERMIAN–TRIASSIC
MASS EXTINCTION?

INOSTRANCEVIA
THERAPSID SYNAPSID
LATE PERMIAN
10 FT. LONG

MOSCHOPS
THERAPSID SYNAPSID
MIDDLE PERMIAN
9 FT. LONG

HERBIVORES THAT
TRAVELED IN HERDS

SYNAPSID SURVIVORS:

Most all synapsids species died in the Permian-Triassic extinction event, and many others were an evolutionary dead end. But there was a subgroup of synapsids called cynodonts that were able to survive. They were a physically small, energetic, and rugged bunch. For example, *Thrinaxodon liorhinus* was an animal about the size of a cat that lived underground. Scientists think the burrowing habit of *T. liorhinus* is what saved the species. Burrowing is a trait that would be passed down to synapsids' evolutionary ancestors—true mammals that would survive multiple future mass extinctions.

THRINAXODON LIORHINUS
THERAPSID SYNAPSID
LATE PERMIAN TO EARLY TRIASSIC
1½ FT. LONG

TRIASSIC EARTH ↘

JURASSIC EARTH ↘

CRETACEOUS EARTH ↗

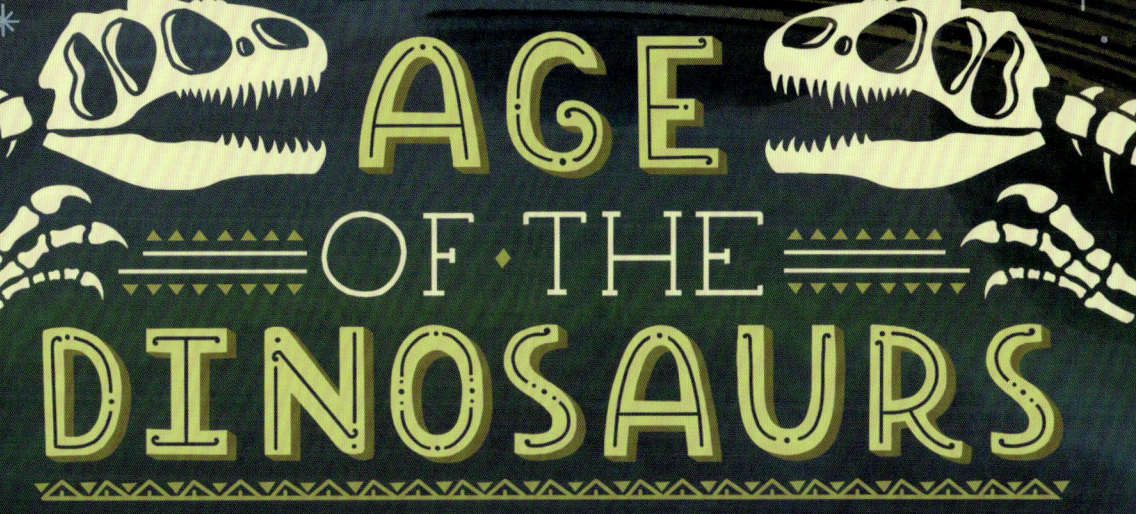

AGE OF THE DINOSAURS

MESOZOIC · ERA

252 MILLION YEARS TO 66 MILLION YEARS AGO

During the **Mesozoic Era** lived the biggest, baddest animals to ever walk the Earth: the dinosaurs. Made up of three periods, the Triassic (252 mya to 201 mya), the Jurassic (201 mya to 145 mya), and the Cretaceous (145 mya to 66 mya), the Mesozoic is all about drama. It was ushered in by the worst mass extinction ever seen and was ended by an asteroid impact with the force of 10 billion atomic bombs. In between catastrophes, dinosaurs would spread across the globe, and in doing so their evolution pushed the boundaries of how large animals could grow on land. Dinosaurs boasted the strongest bites, the tallest reach, and the largest appetites. While the dinosaurs ruled the land, enormous pterosaurs filled the skies and gigantic marine reptiles swam the seas. It was life to the extreme.

It's hard to comprehend the length of 186 million years, and pop culture and movies often depict inaccurate hodgepodges of dinosaurs from different periods. A fictional but familiar scene may show the Cretaceous fan-favorite *Tyrannosaurus rex* fighting a Jurassic *Stegosaurus*. In reality, *T. rex* lived closer in time (by about 16 million years) to the first automobile than to a *Stegosaurus*, whose bones would be long fossilized by the time *T. rex* was on the hunt.

Mesozoic in Greek means "the middle life." The planet was hot, with no polar ice caps. Earth rotated a bit faster than it does now, making a day last only 23 hours. This era is when many modern animal groups and ecosystems took shape. Ancestors of today's birds, also known as avian dinosaurs, first took flight, while the first true mammals burrowed underground. By the end of the Mesozoic, modern flowers bloomed. This is the world that dinosaurs ruled.

GEOLOGICAL TIME SCALE

538.8 MYA

 252 MYA
 201 MYA
 145 MYA
 66 MYA

NOW

PHANEROZOIC EON

MESOZOIC ERA

TRIASSIC PERIOD | JURASSIC PERIOD | CRETACEOUS PERIOD

POSTOSUCHUS

DESMATOSUCHUS

PLACERIAS

COELOPHYSIS

SMILOSUCHUS

THE TRIASSIC PERIOD

252 MILLION YEARS TO 201 MILLION YEARS AGO

Triassic life emerged after the Great Dying, also known as the Permian–Triassic mass extinction event. Close to 90 percent of all animal species were wiped out. The ecological devastation from this disaster would last millions of years, but with time the survivors would eventually flourish. With less competition, many new species and animal groups emerged, adapting to fill the open ecological niches. This rapid evolution is called adaptive radiation and often follows extinction events.

Frogs! Turtles! Mammals! These are just a few of the modern animal groups that evolved during the Triassic. The rulers of this new frontier would be an entire branch of reptiles called the archosaurs, made up of three main groups: in the air were the flying pterosaurs and on land were the pseudosuchians (crocodile-related reptiles) and the dinosaurs. The dinosaurs were not yet the giants made familiar by pop culture. Instead, they were much smaller and hid in the humid forests of Pangea, dodging attacks from the more successful crocodile-like predators.

The Triassic Period would end the way it began, with another mass extinction. This time, disaster was caused by tectonic plate activity as the supercontinent Pangea broke apart. Earthquakes and volcanic explosions that spewed poisonous gasses meant destruction for the majority of Triassic life. But the scrappy dinosaurs were able to survive, adapt, and thrive.

DREPANOSAURUS

ARAUCARIOXYLON ARIZONICUM

TAWA HALLAE

ANASCHISMA

VANCLEAVEA

ARGANODUS

CHINLEA

THE TRIASSIC PERIOD
LIFE ON LAND

The Triassic Period was swelteringly hot. The supercontinent Pangea sat right on Earth's equator, and the atmosphere was heated by greenhouse gasses. The landscape was filled with scorching deserts that were way too hot for a primitive dinosaur to survive. The temperate regions of Earth had more hospitable, humid tropical forests, but the weather was extreme. Unpredictable, global mega-monsoons caused dangerous flash floods.

Weather aside, dinosaurs were simply not the dominant animal group during the Triassic. Early true dinosaurs were small carnivores like *Herrerasaurus* and *Eoraptor*. They darted around on their hind legs and made a living in the middle of the food chain. Meanwhile, crocodile-like pseudosuchians took up many ecological niches. An apex predator like *Saurosuchus* was 18 feet long, and its gigantic snapping croc-like mouth easily chewed up puny dinosaurs.

One of the main Triassic herbivores was the dicynodonts, which were a group of the stem-mammal synapsids. Dicynodonts like the ox-sized *Ischigualastia* dug up plants with their tusks. By the Late Triassic Period, a new herbivore dinosaur group evolved: prosauropods like *Plateosaurus* used their long necks to eat leaves that squat dicynodonts had trouble reaching. Although dinosaurs were often outcompeted and shared the stage with other animal groups during the Triassic, it was just their beginning!

FUN FACTS:

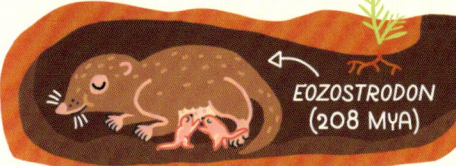

The earliest true mammals emerged during the Triassic. They were the size of rats, lived in burrows, laid eggs like a platypus, and fed their young with milk.

MORGANUCODON (205 MYA)

EOZOSTRODON (208 MYA)

WOW!

PETRIFICATION TURNED THIS WOOD INTO ROCK MADE OF SILICA.

The Petrified Forest National Park in Arizona is famous for fossilized conifer trees from the Triassic.

The Triassic was filled with strange-looking small reptiles like *Sharovipteryx*, which used the skin between its legs to glide.

NAME MEANS "GHOST."

The pseudosuchian *Effigia* was discovered on the property of New Mexico's Ghost Ranch, where famous painter Georgia O'Keeffe worked.

STORIES OF DISCOVERY:

VICTORINO HERRERA

JOSÉ BONAPARTE AND OSVALDO REIG

ISCHIGUALASTIA →

HYPERODAPEDON →

HERRERASAURUS

— MOST OF THE FOSSILS FOUND AT ISCHIGUALASTO BELONG TO DICYNODONTS AND A GROUP OF SMALL PLANT-EATING REPTILES CALLED *RHYNCHOSAURS*.

The Ischigualasto Formation in Argentina in the spot known as Valle de la Luna (Valley of the Moon) is famous for its windswept erosion and colorful rocks. It's also one of the best places to find Triassic fossils. More than 230 mya, this part of Pangea was filled with rivers that attracted animals. Paleontologists hypothesize that flash floods would often bury unsuspecting visitors—not great if you're a dinosaur getting a drink, but perfect conditions for fossilization. Fossil collecting from the Ischigualasto Formation started in the 1940s.

In 1961, with the help of a rancher Victorino Herrera, Argentinian paleontologists Osvaldo Reig and José Bonaparte uncovered one of the earliest true theropod dinosaurs from 237 mya. They named the dinosaur *Herrerasaurus*, in honor of their guide. Theropods are a group of bipedal carnivorous dinosaurs that would eventually include *Tyrannosaurus*, *Velociraptor*, and birds. Dinosaurs only make up a small percentage of the fossils in the Ischigualasto Formation, where an entire fossilized ecosystem has been uncovered. This discovery led scientists to understand the small role dinosaurs played during the Triassic.

THE TRIASSIC PERIOD
AIR AND SEA

Life took millions of years to bounce back from the Permian-Triassic mass extinction event, and the oceans slowly filled with swaying sea lilies called *Encrinus*, cephalopods, and shelled gastropods. During the Triassic, a group of terrestrial reptiles returned to living in the water like their Devonian ancestors. These marine reptiles were not able to re-evolve gills and could not breathe underwater, so they would surface for air like today's whales and dolphins. Some marine reptiles stayed in shallows, like *Lariosaurus*, which filled an ecological niche similar to that of modern seals. Others were open-ocean predators like *Thalattoarchon*, which was nearly the size of a bus. Some were just weird like *Tanystropheus*—its neck was so disproportionately long for its body that scientists think it hunted by lying on the beach while fishing with its head.

The Triassic skies also filled with new creatures. Pterosaurs, a group of archosaur reptiles, became the very first vertebrates to master flight. Pterosaurs evolved wings made of a thin skin membrane that started at the tips of an extremely long finger and stretched to their hind legs. When pterosaurs landed on the ground, they folded their wings to move on all fours.

FUN FACTS:

PSEPHODERMA →
↗ HENODUS

Animals like *Henodus* (237 mya to 228 mya) and *Psephoderma* (215 mya to 201 mya) had shells like turtles!

Early pterosaurs like *Eudimorphodon* (215 mya to 201 mya) and *Peteinosaurus* (215 mya to 212 mya) were the length of a modern fox. They had jagged teeth and likely ate bugs.

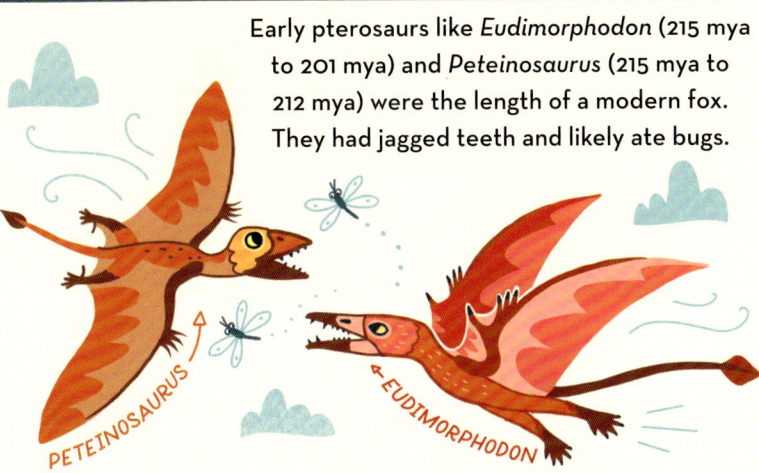

PETEINOSAURUS
← EUDIMORPHODON

The marine reptile *Atopodentatus unicus* (247 mya to 242 mya) was a herbivore whose mouth had a unique shape.

TEETH

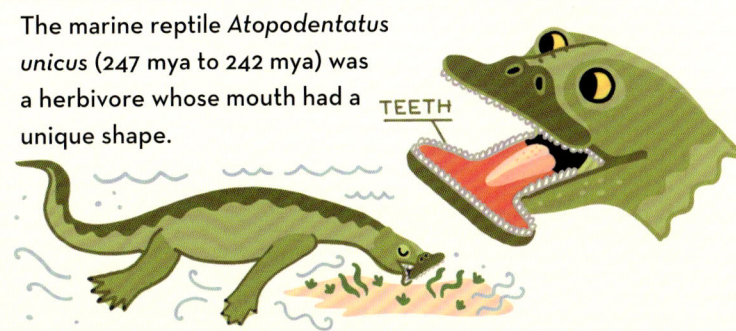

STORIES OF DISCOVERY:

SHONISAURUS ♂
SHONISAURUS
BABY SHONISAURUS

Underneath a 19th-century ghost town in the Nevada desert lies a Triassic graveyard. Berlin-Ichthyosaur State Park is home to an abandoned silver mine and some of the largest Ichthyosaur marine reptile fossils ever found. Excavation began in 1954, and since then forty ichthyosaur skeletons have been uncovered, ranging from 2 to 50 feet long. One dig site contains seven adult skeletons of the species *Shonisaurus popularis*, which are each the size of a modern gray whale. Despite their size, *Shonisaurus* fossils are extremely rare. What brought these animals together?

In 2022, paleontologists used micro X-rays, three-dimensional scans, and digital reconstruction to reexamine the fossils. They learned that many of the adults were pregnant or accompanied by newborns, meaning that 230 mya this was their birthing grounds. Scientists believe that over generations *Shonisaurus* returned to give birth at the same nursery habitat, just as today's whales migrate to do so.

···THE TRIASSIC PERIOD···
CREATURE FEATURE

SILESAURUS OPOLENSIS
SILESAURID DINOSAURIFORM
LATE TRIASSIC
7½ FT. LONG

NOT A TRUE DINOSAUR, BUT RELATED TO AN EARLIER EVOLUTIONARY OFFSHOOT CALLED A DINOSAURIFORM.

LILIENSTERNUS
THEROPOD DINOSAUR
LATE TRIASSIC
15½ TO 20 FT. LONG

ONE OF THE LARGEST DINOSAURS OF THE TRIASSIC

HUNTED OTHER DINOSAURS

YIKES!

NYASASAURUS
MIDDLE TRIASSIC
7 TO 10 FT. LONG

POSSIBLE SAUROPODOMORPH DINOSAUR

DATED 243 MYA, THIS MIGHT BE ONE OF THE EARLIEST DINOSAURS.

IT IS DEBATED WHETHER IT WAS A TRUE DINOSAUR OR A PRIMITIVE DINOSAURIFORM.

HOW DINOSAURS WALK:

The main difference between dinosaurs and other archosaur reptiles is how they walk. Dinosaurs have a hip joint that allows their legs to stand straight underneath their body. In contrast, crocodiles, lizards, and turtles all have their legs positioned out and away from their body, making for a stockier stance and slower gait.

DINOSAUR

CROCODILE

LEGS UPRIGHT AND UNDER BODY

LEGS OUT AND AWAY FROM BODY

MAIN DINOSAUR GROUPS:

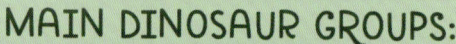

SAURISCHIA
NAME MEANS "LIZARD HIPPED."

ORNITHISCHIA
NAME MEANS "BIRD HIPPED."

THEROPODS
ARE TWO-LEGGED CARNIVORES.

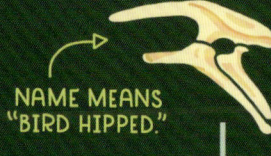
SAUROPODOMORPHS
ARE LONG-NECKED HERBIVORES.

ORNITHISCHIANS
ARE HERBIVORES.

The shape of the hip bone (also known as the pubis) would define the two main dinosaur groups.

PLATEOSAURUS TROSSINGENSIS

SAUROPODOMORPH DINOSAUR
LATE TRIASSIC

JAWS HAD ROUGH
SERRATED TEETH FOR
GRINDING AND
TEARING PLANTS.

PROSAUROPODS ARE SOME
OF THE EARLIEST PLANT-
EATING DINOSAURS.

◁--- 20 TO 33 FT. LONG ---▷

TAIL MADE UP
OVER HALF OF
ITS LENGTH.

Prosauropods are the ancestors to Jurassic Period sauropods like *Brontosaurus*, which are famous for their long-necked silhouette and giant four-legged bodies. The much earlier prosauropods from the Triassic, like *Plateosaurus*, were smaller and walked on their hind legs to reach food. Their arms were primarily used to grab branches for munching leaves. *Plateosaurus* even had partially opposable thumbs to better grasp their snacks. Paleontologists have found more than fifty complete skeletons in dig sites in Germany, Greenland, and beneath the North Sea, making *Plateosaurus* one of the best understood dinosaurs. Scientists believe that plateosauruses traveled in large groups and possibly migrated to find food, like herds of modern giraffes.

MORE PROSAUROPOD DINOSAURS

THECODONTOSAURUS
SAUROPODOMORPH DINOSAUR
LATE TRIASSIC
3¼ TO 9¾ FT. LONG

SATURNALIA
SAUROPODOMORPH DINOSAUR
LATE TRIASSIC
6½ FT. LONG

FOUND IN
BRAZIL

FOUND INSIDE
ANCIENT CAVES
IN BRISTOL,
ENGLAND, IN
1834

THE JURASSIC PERIOD

201 MILLION YEARS TO 145 MILLION YEARS AGO

Before the Jurassic Period, trouble was brewing deep under the Earth's surface. The supercontinent Pangea was slowly tearing apart. As tectonic plates moved, volcanoes erupted and spewed lava and greenhouses gasses. The Triassic–Jurassic mass extinction event wiped out more than 76 percent of all animal species. Crocodile-like pseudosuchians that once outcompeted the dinosaurs were nearly all gone by the start of the Jurassic— only a small group survived, eventually evolving into modern alligators and crocodiles. Somehow, in all the chaos of mass extinction, the dinosaurs emerged pretty much unscathed. Why dinosaurs survived is still a mystery. Perhaps dinosaurs reproduced at a higher rate than the pseudosuchians. Maybe being less specialized gave early dinosaurs an advantage. Whatever the reasons, dinosaurs found themselves with little competition and room to spread out.

Pangea separated into two distinct halves, Laurasia and Gondwana, creating new shallow-water habitats. The deserts of the Triassic Period shrank and were replaced with lush Jurassic rainforests. These rainforests were an all-you-can-eat buffet that would fuel new supersized dinosaurs.

APATOSAURUS

BRACHIOSAURUS

DIPLODOCUS

THE JURASSIC PERIOD
LIFE ON LAND

The Jurassic landscape was rich with plant life. The forests were covered with ginkgo trees, evergreen conifers, and palm tree–like cycads. The ground was carpeted with lush ferns, mosses, and horsetails. Plants also had new helpers: insect pollinators! Fossils of moth ancestors have been found in the remains of 200-million-year-old pond scum in Germany. Real flowers would evolve millions of years later during the Cretaceous Period, but a group of now-extinct plants called Bennettitales had proto-flower structures that produced nectar and pollen. As dinosaurs lumbered about during the Jurassic, a fluttering insect called *Oregramma illecebrosa* may have drunk the nectar from a *Williamsonia* plant while unwittingly spreading pollen. Many scientists believe that as early as the Jurassic, all kinds of species of beetles and flies started to coevolve with plants, transforming the evolutionary future for them both.

Sprawling forests meant enough food to fuel herbivores to grow mythically large. Long-necked, leaf-munching sauropods are a group of dinosaurs that were the largest land animals ever. Many different species of sauropods coexisted in a single forest, with each species specialized to reach and chew a different kind of plant. Below them, sharing the bounty, were plant-eating ornithischian dinosaurs like *Camptosaurus* and the armored *Stegosaurus*. The abundance of supersized prey animals meant supersized predators. Theropods like *Megalosaurus* and *Ceratosaurus* grew to 25 feet long. The even bigger *Allosaurus* would charge its prey while running on its hind legs. Life in the Jurassic was big, bold, and hungry!

FUN FACTS:

Modern ginkgo trees are living fossils, meaning that they are extremely similar to the trees of the Jurassic!

In the late 1800s, two wealthy paleontologists, Othniel Marsh and Edward Cope, were competitive rivals.

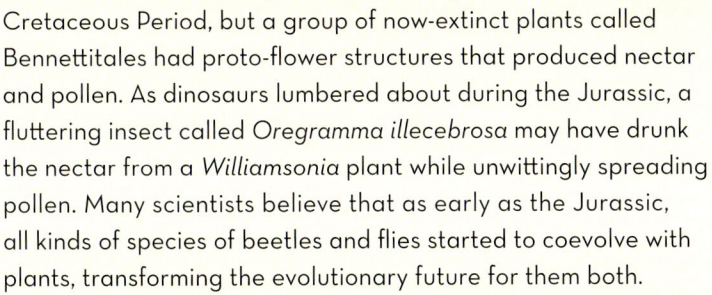

MARSH COPE

THEIR FIGHT WAS CALLED "THE BONE WARS."

BOOM.

OVER 130 SPECIES OF DINOSAURS WERE DISCOVERED AS THEY COMPETED.

They each used their fortune to hire teams to dig up fossils in the Jurassic Morrison Formation of the western United States. Their famous feud led to fights, stealing from one another, breaking fossils, sabotage, and the eventual disgrace of them both.

← ITS NECK HAS 19 VERTEBRAE AND IS 43 FT. LONG!

The sauropod *Mamenchisaurus* (160 mya) found in China has the longest neck of any known animal.

STORIES OF DISCOVERY:

As cowboys galloped through the Wild West of Utah, under their feet was the densest deposit of meat-eating dinosaur fossils in the world. No one knows for sure when the carnivore death-pit was discovered, because there were so many bones freely exposed from erosion. Since 1929 excavations have been carried out continuously. More than 12,000 dinosaur bones have been found in the Cleveland-Lloyd Dinosaur Quarry, and more than 75 percent of them belonged to carnivores like *Allosaurus*. What led so many apex predators to die in one location has eluded scientists. Geologists have analyzed the rocks and know this spot was once a seasonal watering hole. Some hypothesize that animals got stuck in the mud when it dried up each year, but this still leaves many questions unanswered as to what killed so many allosauruses. Only new discoveries will solve this mystery.

THE CLEVELAND LLOYD DINOSAUR QUARRY PROVIDES *ALLOSAURUS* SKELETONS TO MORE THAN 60 MUSEUMS AROUND THE WORLD!

AWESOME!

THE JURASSIC PERIOD
AIR AND SEA

At the very start of the Jurassic, the oceans had a new sparkling form of life: teeny single-celled diatoms. This new kind of microscopic algae, with cell walls made of silica, looked like tiny shimmering jewels that formed beautiful geometric shapes, zigzags, and ribbons. Like all algae, diatoms get their energy from the sun through photosynthesis. Today, diatoms produce 20 to 50 percent of Earth's oxygen. The earliest-known diatom fossil dates to 182 mya, but there is evidence that their origin could be millions of years earlier. From the Jurassic to today, diatoms have been an essential base of the ocean's food web.

Zooming out from the microscopic, gigantic marine animals also thrived during the Jurassic. Ichthyosaurs like *Nannopterygius*, gigantic fishes, and sharks all filled the open sea. They would have had to swim fast to escape the 16-foot-long crocodylomorph *Dakosaurus*, nicknamed the Godzilla of the ocean. Above the seas and jungles, pterosaurs spread out to fill the skies. By the Late Jurassic, pterosaurs like the long-tailed *Rhamphorhynchus* lived on the coasts and hunted fishes. Gigantic and tiny, above and below, the Jurassic oceans, shores, and skies were teeming with life!

FUN FACTS:

I CAN SEE YOU!

The ichthyosaurus *Ophthalmosaurus* had a gigantic eye for hunting at night and in dark ocean depths.

Anurognathus was a bug-eating pterosaur that was smaller than your hand.

I'M SUPER CUTE!

ANUROGNATHUS 3½ IN. LONG

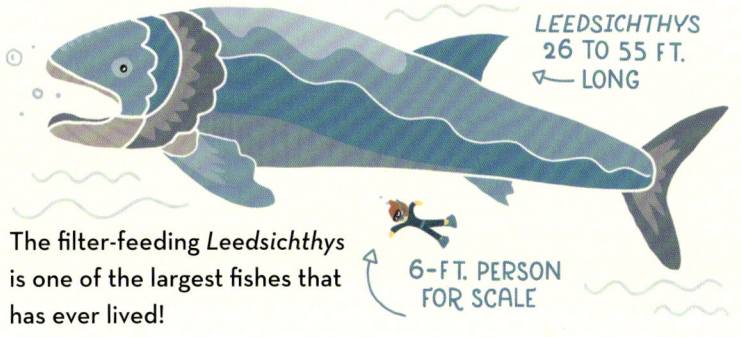

LEEDSICHTHYS 26 TO 55 FT. LONG

The filter-feeding *Leedsichthys* is one of the largest fishes that has ever lived!

6-FT. PERSON FOR SCALE

STORIES OF DISCOVERY:

A 12-year-old girl named Mary Anning would discover some of the first marine reptiles. In the English seaside of the Lyme Regis, Anning climbed dangerous cliffs in search of fossils that she sold to tourists to help feed her family. At the time, the public thought fossils were just trinkets, and some even considered fossils mystical oddities, calling them snake stones and devil's toenails. Anning wanted to know more about her findings. She took copious notes in her journal and even arranged the fossilized bones together. Around 1811, she discovered and identified a complete ichthyosaur skeleton of a *Stenopterygius*. In 1823, she found the first complete *Plesiosaurus* and in 1828 a fossilized *Pterodactylus*. Her discoveries helped prove that animals could go extinct and provided evidence of the age of the reptiles. Women, especially those of Anning's low social standing, were not allowed to publish at the time. Male scientists flocked to her work and took credit for her discoveries. Now, Mary Anning is rightfully celebrated as the Mother of Paleontology.

MARY ANNING IS A POSTHUMOUS HONORARY MEMBER OF THE GEOLOGICAL SOCIETY OF LONDON.

SHE BROUGHT HER DOG ALONG ON FOSSIL DIGS!

AIR-FILLED CREST ON HEAD →

GUANLONG
THEROPOD DINOSAUR
LATE JURASSIC
10 FT. LONG

NAME MEANS "CROWNED DRAGON."

HAD BONY PLATES CALLED SCUTES FROM NECK TO TAIL

CERATOSAURUS →
THEROPOD DINOSAUR
LATE JURASSIC
20 FT. LONG

DILOPHOSAURUS
FACE CREST USED TO ATTRACT A MATE →

3 HORNS →

RAAARR.

EXTRA-LONG BLADE-LIKE TEETH

CRYOLOPHOSAURUS
THEROPOD DINOSAUR
EARLY JURASSIC
21 FT. LONG

RUN!

THEROPOD DINOSAUR
EARLY JURASSIC
23 FT. LONG

NICKNAMED ELVISAURUS FOR ITS CREST THAT LOOKS LIKE THE SINGER ELVIS'S HAIRDO

FIERCE PREDATORS:

The Jurassic Period had some of the fiercest predators to ever roam the Earth, the most famous of which is *Allosaurus*. Surprisingly, this giant monster did not have a powerful jaw but instead an incredibly strong head. Instead of biting, paleontologists think it would keep its mouth open to slash its prey, using its sharp teeth like an axe.

HATCHET-LIKE MOUTH →

DOZENS OF SERRATED TEETH

WHACK

ALLOSAURUS ↗
THEROPOD DINOSAUR
LATE JURASSIC
30 FT. LONG

DISCOVERED
IN LIAONING,
CHINA, IN 2011

XIAOTINGIA

THEROPOD DINOSAUR
LATE JURASSIC, 167 MYA
24 IN. LONG

ARCHAEOPTERYX

THEROPOD DINOSAUR
LATE JURASSIC, 150 MYA
20 IN. LONG

SHARP
TEETH

BONY
TAIL

FIRST DISCOVERED IN
GERMANY IN 1861

THE FIRST BIRD IS A DINOSAUR:

One of the earliest-known avian dinosaurs to be directly linked
to all modern birds is *Archaeornithura meemannae*, which dates
back to 130 mya. Even earlier than that lived bird-like dinosaurs
that straddle the line between avian and non-avian dinosaurs.

  Archaeopteryx was once considered one of the oldest-known
members of the bird family, until the discovery of even older
bird-like dinosaurs like *Xiaotingia*. Covered in feathers, these
dinosaurs flew across the Jurassic skies and were about the size
of a modern crow. These transitional species had traits from
two different groups of animals and represent an important
evolutionary step between non-avian dinosaurs and modern
birds. Like many transitionary species, there is much debate
about what group they truly belong to.

ALL ARE THEROPOD
DINOSAURS.

& BIRDS

TYRANNOSAURUS

VELOCIRAPTOR

All birds (also known as avian dinosaurs) are members of the
larger theropod dinosaur group, which also includes non-avian
predators like *Allosaurus*, *Tyrannosaurus*, and *Velociraptor*.

···THE JURASSIC PERIOD···
CREATURE FEATURE

SCELIDOSAURUS
ORNITHISCHIAN DINOSAUR
EARLY JURASSIC
13 FT. LONG

LIGHTLY ARMORED
WITH SMALL, BONY
DEFENSIVE PLATES

A PRIMITIVE
ANKYLOSAUR

GARGOYLEOSAURUS
ORNITHISCHIAN DINOSAUR
LATE JURASSIC
13 FT. LONG

AN EARLY MEMBER OF
THE ANKYLOSAUR GROUP

SHORT
SPIKES FOR
DEFENSE

HUAYANGOSAURUS
ORNITHISCHIAN DINOSAUR
MIDDLE JURASSIC
15 FT. LONG

A CLOSE RELATIVE TO
THE STEGOSAURUS THAT
WAS HALF ITS SIZE

PRIMITIVE
MEMBER OF THE
STEGOSAURIA
FAMILY

KENTROSAURUS
ORNITHISCHIAN DINOSAUR
LATE JURASSIC
15 FT. LONG

DISCOVERED
IN TANZANIA

ARMORED DINOSAURS:

Stegosaurus is famous for its dazzling back plates and is often depicted using them to fight off hungry predators, but paleontologists think that this is an unlikely scenario. The diamond-shaped plates on the back of a *Stegosaurus* were probably used as a courtship display. In contrast, the 3-foot-long tail spikes also found on the *Stegosaurus* and its relatives were definitely used as defensive weapons.

STEGOSAURUS
ORNITHISCHIAN DINOSAUR
LATE JURASSIC
30 FT. LONG

PLATES FOR
COURTSHIP

WOW!

SPIKES FOR
DEFENSE

WHACK!

OW!

HOW TO FUEL A GIANT:

Sauropods are one of the largest groups of dinosaurs, both in size and number of species. How did they get so big? First, they needed to eat a lot of food. Each sauropod's long neck was specialized to reach as much food as possible with minimal body movement. Their size also required a more efficient way to breathe. Sauropod lungs took in oxygen when both inhaling and exhaling. This is called a unidirectional lung, which contains extra expanding air sacs for storing oxygen. All birds today have unidirectional lungs, which helps fuel their high-energy flying lifestyle. For sauropods, these extra air sacs also helped them cool down, acting like an internal air conditioner, which was necessary to prevent their humongous bodies from overheating. Scientists think all dinosaurs had unidirectional lungs.

BRACHIOSAURUS
SAUROPOD DINOSAUR
LATE JURASSIC

CHISEL-SHAPED TEETH

SAUROPODS DID NOT CHEW; INSTEAD THEY SWALLOWED FOOD WHOLE.

ATE 440 LBS. OF PLANT MATTER A DAY

← - - 75 FT. LONG - - →

6 FT. 7 IN. TALL

6 FT. TALL

A PERSON COMPARED TO A *BRACHIOSAURUS'S* HUMERUS LEG BONE.

WEIGHS 55 TONS— THAT'S HEAVIER THAN A HUMPBACK WHALE!

BABY SAUROPODS GROW AT A FAST RATE. BABIES START OUT THE SIZE OF A SQUIRREL AND GROW INTO GIANT ADULTS IN 20 TO 30 YEARS.

SPECIALIZED SAUROPODS!

More than 300 species of sauropods have been discovered from throughout the Mesozoic Era. The Morrison Formation in the western United States contains twenty-four species of sauropod fossils, all from the Late Jurassic. Many of these giants coexisted at the same time, but how did these big boys not all fight over food? An evolutionary trick called niche partitioning meant that different species avoided competition by becoming specialized. These sauropods all ate different plants! Their necks' reach and tooth shapes provide clues about each species' favorite meal.

BRACHIOSAURUS' CHISEL-SHAPED TEETH GRABBED TOUGH LEAVES.

DIPLODOCUS SKULL→

APATOSAURUS AND DIPLODOCUS HAD PEG-LIKE TEETH FOR STRIPPING SMALL LEAVES FROM BRANCHES.

←BRACHIOSAURUS

←APATOSAURUS

←DIPLODOCUS

THE CRETACEOUS PERIOD

145 MILLION YEARS TO 66 MILLION YEARS AGO

The Cretaceous Period was the grand finale of the Mesozoic Era. Ornately feathered raptors prowled between trees that now bloomed with flowers. *Tyrannosaurus*, with its powerful jaws, was the apex predator of forests. In the sky, the azhdarchid pterosaurs grew to be the largest flying animals of all time. And many birds—which surprisingly wouldn't look out of place today—flew about and landed on large dinosaurs to eat flies. Out in the sea, carnivorous marine reptiles like *Mosasaurus* grew to the size of modern whales.

What divides the Cretaceous from the Jurassic is not a messy mass die-off or natural disaster, but instead is a line of white chalk in the fossil record. As the supercontinents Gondwana and Laurasia continued to drift apart and sea levels rose, many new shallow waterways formed, which were perfect for algae blooms to thrive. Their fossilized remains made of calcium carbonate turned the rock from this period into bright white chalk, and it's what gives the Cretaceous its name (*creta* is Latin for "chalk"). By the end of the Cretaceous Period, you could even start to make out the outlines of our modern continents.

The dinosaurs had been successful for more than 200 million years. It seemed inevitable that they would lumber into another epoch, but sometimes life on Earth can change overnight.

ACHERORAPTOR

THE CRETACEOUS PERIOD
LIFE ON LAND

A revolution took place among plant life: the emergence of flowers! Early Cretaceous flowers were small and first bloomed on water lilies and wintergreens. Fossil evidence of the very first true flower is from 130 mya. By the end of this period, flowering trees like magnolias bloomed worldwide. Dinosaurs, like the duck-billed *Edmontosaurus*, developed specialized teeth-lined jaws for mowing down all this new plant food. As pollen filled the air, these flowering plants continued to spread with the help of insect pollinators, including the ancestors of modern bees, beetles, and moths.

There was more biodiversity and unique dinosaur species than ever before! The continents were fully separated by oceans, blocking the migration of dinosaurs. When members of the same species are separated by a physical barrier, they can evolve into completely different species. This is an evolutionary process known as allopatric speciation. Over time this isolation can cause landlocked ecosystems to contain wildly different plants and animals. For example, the Cretaceous island continent of South America was home to an abundance of long-necked sauropods, while hardly any have been found in North America.

FUN FACTS:

Feathered dinosaurs lived all over the world, but fossils of some of the most impressive species have been found in China.

SINOSAUROPTERYX→

GALLIMIMUS

← SMALL BUT HAD LONG SPIKES?

AMARGASAURUS
EARLY CRETACEOUS
33 FT. LONG

ARGENTINOSAURUS
LATE CRETACEOUS
130 FT. LONG

Some of the wildest-looking and tallest sauropods lived during the Cretaceous Period. South America is where many sauropods of record-breaking size have been discovered.

Spinosaurus, famous for its frilled back, was a gigantic predator that lived 98 mya in the tropical swamps of what is now Africa.

STORIES OF DISCOVERY:

IGUANODON

← THE CRYSTAL PALACE DINOSAURS
CONSTRUCTED IN 1853-1855 →

MEGALOSAURUS→

HYLAEOSAURUS→

SIZE, SHAPE, AND EVEN THE PLACEMENT OF HORNS WAS FAR OFF.

IGUANODON NOW

IGUANODON THEN

OTHER SCULPTURES AT THE CRYSTAL PALACE INCLUDED ICHTHYOSAURS, PTERODACTYLS, AND A GIANT GROUND SLOTH.

In 1851, the Crystal Palace was built in London to host the World's Fair to celebrate technological innovations of the Victorian age. But how to decorate the surrounding gardens? With animals of the ancient past! That was the thinking when artist Benjamin Waterhouse Hawkins was hired to create dinosaur sculptures. In 1842, the reptile fossils of *Megalosaurus*, *Iguanodon*, and *Hylaeosaurus* were categorized by paleontologist Sir Richard Owen in a brand new animal group named Dinosauria. With Owen's expertise, Hawkins created giant sculptures based on living monitor lizards and crocodiles. Today it is clear that these representations were far from correct, but this art was the very first of its kind. The Crystal Palace dinosaurs helped to introduce the Victorian public to prehistoric life. People were in awe! Before attending the World's Fair, officials even dined inside the sculpted body of the *Iguanodon*. Today, science communication and prehistoric art continue to help the public understand what a fossil represents. Public excitement helps get research funded and inspires a future generation of scientists!

THE CRETACEOUS PERIOD
AIR AND SEA

Avian dinosaurs (also known as birds) had more than 80 million years of adaptation since they first evolved in the Jurassic Period. Birds diversified into many ecological niches, and some looked so familiar that they wouldn't seem out of place today. For example, waterfowl like *Vegavis* flew around Antarctica and looked like a modern goose. Most birds in the Cretaceous had teeth on their beaks, like *Janavis*, which likely used them while diving into the ocean to catch fishes. Birds likely competed with pterodactyls for food, risking becoming a meal themselves.

HONK

VEGAVIS
66 MYA

Cretaceous birds were small compared to the pterosaurs that dominated the skies. None were as mighty as a group of gigantic pterosaurs called azhdarchids, many of which rivaled the size of a biplane. The oceans were filled with enormous predators, and a group of marine reptiles called mosasaurs were unique to the Late Cretaceous. *Mosasaurus hoffmannii* was the size of a city bus, while other species were a little bigger than a dolphin. Mosasaurs are closely related to snakes and monitor lizards and can only be described as "nightmare fuel." They hunted sharks, plesiosaurs, and even smaller mosasaurs.

While some species of fishes and alligators survived the asteroid impact that ended the Mesozoic Era, the giants of the sea and sky—the mosasaurs and the azhdarchids—live on only in our imaginations.

FUN FACTS:

Hesperornis was a flightless seabird that lived like today's penguins.

MANY PRIMITIVE BIRDS HAD TEETH!

18 FT. TALL

One of the largest-known azhdarchids was *Quetzalcoatlus*. It was too big to hunt in the air and instead ran down prey on all fours. It returned to the sky with an 8-foot jump.

PREYED ON DINOSAURS

RUN AWAY!

Pterodaustro had thousands of thin teeth for filtering plankton from the water.

12 FT. LONG

6-FT. HUMAN

The extinct *Archelon* is the largest turtle ever found!

STORIES OF DISCOVERY:

SKULL WAS ABOUT 5 FT. LONG.

OOOH!

59 FT. LONG

FOSSIL WAS FROM A MOSASAURUS HOFFMANNII

Mosasaur fossils have been found on every continent on Earth. One of the earliest discoveries is shrouded in legend and rumors. In 1780, under Mount Saint Peter in the Netherlands, a giant skull was discovered in a chalk quarry. The workers called a retired army doctor to examine the skull, and he declared it was from a giant crocodile (wrong!). Other experts claimed it was from a giant whale (also wrong!). During the French Revolution, the army took a special interest in "the famous skull," and in 1794 French soldiers allegedly stole it and carried it all the way to the Natural History Museum in Paris. Many years later the skull was finally identified properly as a marine lizard. In 1822 it was named *Mosasaurus*, the holotype of this group of extinct animals.

THE CRETACEOUS PERIOD
CREATURE FEATURE

CONFUCIUSORNIS

THEROPOD DINOSAUR
EARLY CRETACEOUS
1 FT. LONG →

FOUND IN CHINA
IN FOSSIL DEPOSITS
OF LIAONING

↑ ONE OF THE EARLIEST
BIRDS WITH A TOOTHLESS
BEAK (125 MYA), ALONG
WITH *EOCONFUCIUSORNIS*
(131 MYA)

VELOCIRAPTOR

SICKLE-
SHAPED
CLAW FOR
SLASHING
PREY →

THEROPOD DINOSAUR
LATE CRETACEOUS
6 FT. LONG

CITIPATI

THEROPOD DINOSAUR
LATE CRETACEOUS
8 FT. LONG →

MICRORAPTOR

WINGS
COULD
GLIDE AND
FLY IN
SHORT
BURSTS.

THEROPOD DINOSAUR
EARLY CRETACEOUS
3 FT. LONG

SITS ON EGGS TO INCUBATE
THEM LIKE A MOTHER HEN

FEATHERED DINOSAURS:

The first feathered dinosaurs and "dino-birds"
had evolved millions of years earlier, during the
Jurassic. By the Cretaceous, many dinosaurs
sported modern feathers. While birds used
their wings to fly, large feathered dinosaurs like
velociraptors used feathers for warmth and
mating displays.

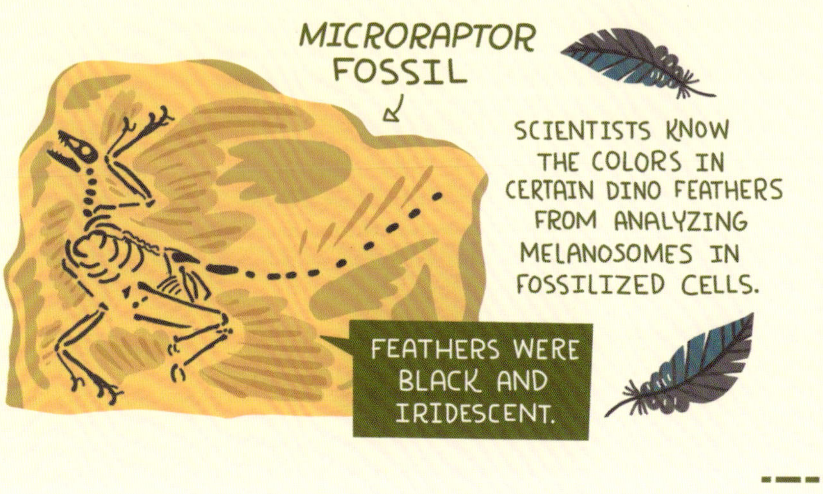

MICRORAPTOR
FOSSIL

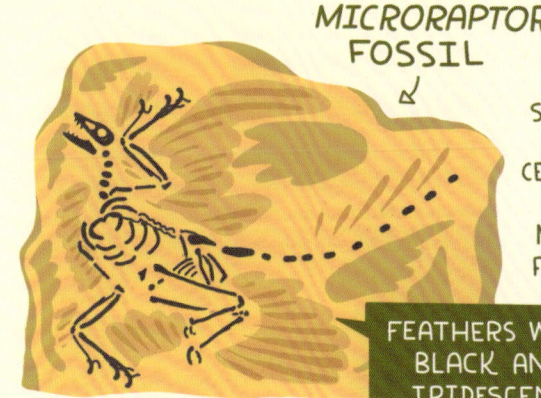

SCIENTISTS KNOW
THE COLORS IN
CERTAIN DINO FEATHERS
FROM ANALYZING
MELANOSOMES IN
FOSSILIZED CELLS.

FEATHERS WERE
BLACK AND
IRIDESCENT.

TYRANNOSAURUS REX

THEROPOD DINOSAUR
LATE CRETACEOUS

←-- 39 FT. LONG --→

↑ 20 FT. TALL

JUVENILE *TYRANNOSAURUS* GREW EXTREMELY FAST, PUTTING ON 1,500 POUNDS EACH YEAR BETWEEN THE AGES OF 13 AND 17.

RAWR!

RUN!

6-TO 12-IN. LONG TEETH

HAD LIPS

Tyrannosaurus rex means "the tyrant lizard king." Onlookers were terrified when the first skeletal reconstruction was displayed in 1915. Even back then, scientists knew its upright stance was incorrect, but this orientation was set by the limitations of the skeleton's steel support structure. This silhouette was cemented in pop culture by multiple monster movies in which *T. rex* had a starring role. Since then, this dinosaur's posture has been corrected.

The bite of *T. rex* is one of the strongest of any animal to ever live on land. It could crush through bones with a force of 1.7 tons! Other members of the Tyrannosauridae family have been found in Asia and North America.

1915

OH MY!

HOW GHASTLY!

TODAY

WOW!

COOL!

OUR UNDERSTANDING OF PREHISTORIC LIFE IS ALWAYS EVOLVING!

THE CRETACEOUS PERIOD
CREATURE FEATURE

CERATOPSIANS

EINIOSAURUS
ORNITHISCHIAN DINOSAUR
LATE CRETACEOUS
15 FT. LONG

CENTROSAURUS

STYRACOSAURUS

PENTACERATOPS

PACHYCEPHALOSAURIA

PACHYCEPHALOSAURUS
ORNITHISCHIAN DINOSAUR
LATE CRETACEOUS
13 FT. LONG

PRENOCEPHALE

STEGOCERAS

FRILLS, HORNS, AND HARD HEADS:

Marginocephalia is a clade of dinosaurs that are defined by having a bony shelf on their skull. The clade is divided even further into two subgroups: the extremely thick-skulled pachycephalosaurians and the horned and ornately frilled ceratopsians.

There are more than seventy species of ceratopsian, but the most famous is *Triceratops*. Ceratopsians' large head frills developed as they matured to attract potential mates, just like antlers on an elk. Their horns were used for defense and to fight for social dominance and territory. Fossilized horns show evidence that ceratopsians of the same species often locked horns in battle—even to the point of breaking.

Pachycephalosauria is a smaller two-legged dinosaur group that used their incredibly thick skulls to headbutt opponents. Like modern rams, they would butt heads for dominance or to defend themselves.

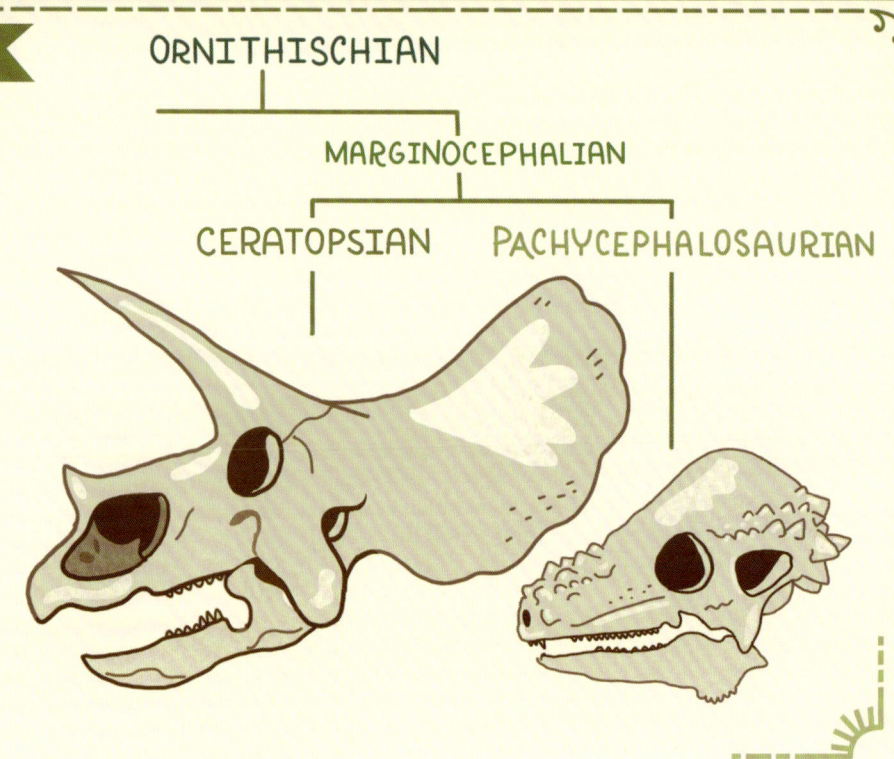

ORNITHISCHIAN

MARGINOCEPHALIAN

CERATOPSIAN   PACHYCEPHALOSAURIAN

PARASAUROLOPHUS WALKERI

ORNITHISCHIAN DINOSAUR
LATE CRETACEOUS

ITS CREST GREW
6 FT. TALL.

←--- 33 FT. LONG ---→

JAWS HAD
HUNDREDS
OF TEETH IN
ROWS TO GRIND
PLANTS INTO
A PULP.

CRESTS THAT MAKE NOISE:

Hadrosauridae, a family known as duck-billed dinosaurs, were some of the most prolific plant eaters of the Late Cretaceous. Many species, like *Parasaurolophus* shown above, had impressive crests. These crests were hollow and contained a resonating chamber that allowed the animals to make loud, billowing sounds, like a horn. Perhaps these animals bellowed out a boastful call to attract mates or used their instrument to communicate and signal to the rest of the herd, just like elephants do today.

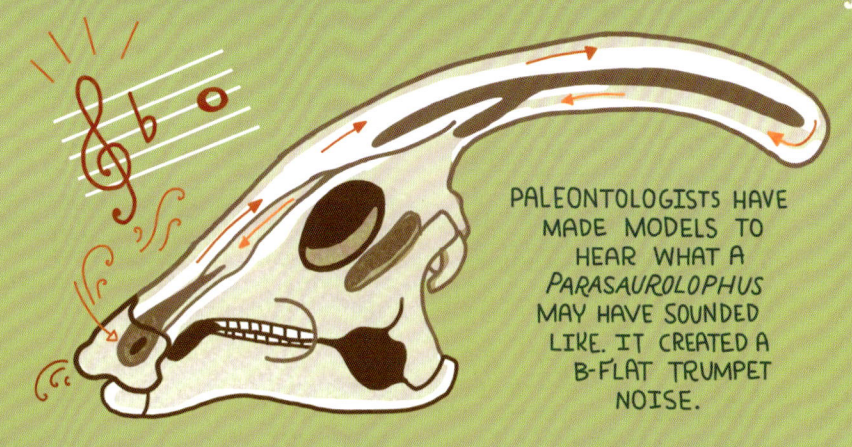

PALEONTOLOGISTS HAVE
MADE MODELS TO
HEAR WHAT A
PARASAUROLOPHUS
MAY HAVE SOUNDED
LIKE. IT CREATED A
B-FLAT TRUMPET
NOISE.

MORE HADROSAURIDAE FROM THE LATE CRETACEOUS

CORYTHOSAURUS

←HELMET-
LIKE CREST

SOUNDED LIKE
A FOGHORN

SAUROLOPHUS

FOUND IN ASIA AND
NORTH AMERICA

LAMBEOSAURUS

MALES AND FEMALES
HAD DIFFERENT-
SHAPED CRESTS.

The last day of the Mesozoic Era was like any other. Pterosaurs soared in the sky, while *Triceratops* bulls clashed horns. Dinosaurs were thriving, and then disaster struck. Then, 66 mya, an asteroid larger than Mount Everest collided with Earth in the Yucatán Peninsula of Mexico. The force of the impact created a wall of flames and 600-mile-per-hour winds, annihilating everything within a 900-mile radius. The explosion caused shockwaves, global earthquakes, and massive tsunamis. The asteroid completely vaporized on impact, shooting molten rock and debris into space. This material cooled into millions of tiny glass balls called tektites. Trapped in Earth's gravity, tektites rained down like bullets, super-heating the air. Wildfires blazed worldwide, and the animals that somehow survived the initial destruction were left with little to eat. Entire ecosystems collapsed, and 80 percent of all animal species went extinct. Large dinosaurs, pterosaurs, and marine reptiles all disappeared.

EVIDENCE LEFT BEHIND:

Evidence of the Cretaceous–Paleogene mass extinction event is found throughout the world in the fossil record, marked as a dark line in the rock called the K-Pg boundary. This dark rock layer contains a high percentage of iridium, a type of metal found in asteroids. Sphere-shaped tektites formed from the impact are also found in this layer of rock. Using radiometric dating, scientists have confirmed that the K-Pg boundary is about 66 million years old. Before this line there is an abundance of non-avian dinosaur fossils, and after it there are none.

ABOVE THE K-PG BOUNDARY, NO MORE NON-AVIAN DINOSAUR FOSSILS.

IRIDIUM

TEKTITES

BROKEN QUARTZ

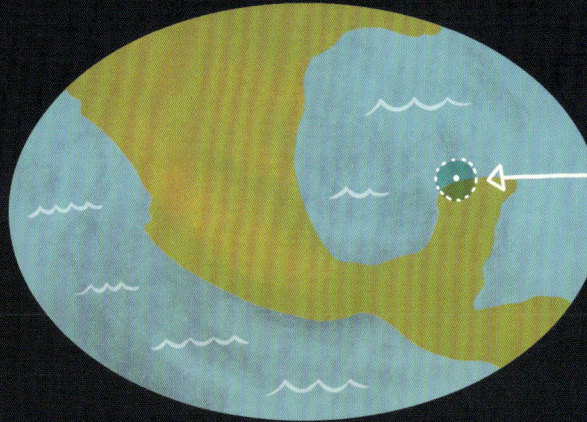

The asteroid left behind a crater 112 miles across near what is now Chicxulub Pueblo, Mexico.

In North Dakota, there is a dig site called Tanis with fossils from the day the asteroid hit. While dinosaurs at the asteroid's impact site were vaporized, Tanis was an ancient riverbank far enough away to allow species to be fossilized. The animals died from violent floods caused by the asteroid's shockwaves. It is like a crime scene with clues that uncover what life was like right before and during the mass extinction event.

DINOSAUR FOOTPRINTS

LEG OF A DINOSAUR THAT LIKELY DIED IN THE SHOCKWAVES

FISH WITH TEKTITES IN GILLS

WHO SURVIVED:

Despite global destruction, there were animals and plants that withstood the harsh conditions. While most dinosaurs perished, a few species of ground-dwelling birds survived. Other animal groups that made it included alligators, crocodiles, lizards, fishes, frogs, turtles, salamanders, and most arthropods. Hearty plants like gingko trees, redwoods, and many flowering plants also pulled through. The most important survivor to humanity is a small group of mouse-sized mammals that hid underground. Their small size and opportunistic diet helped them hold out while food was scarce. The extinction of large dinosaurs paved the way for the rise of the mammals.

LIVING UNDERGROUND, SMALL SIZE, AND AN OPPORTUNIST DIET HELPED THESE ANIMALS SURVIVE.

AVIAN DINOSAURS THAT SURVIVED MOST LIKELY RESEMBLED GROUND-DWELLING QUAILS.

PALEOGENE EARTH

NEOGENE EARTH

QUATERNARY EARTH,
LAST GLACIAL MAXIMUM

QUATERNARY EARTH, TODAY

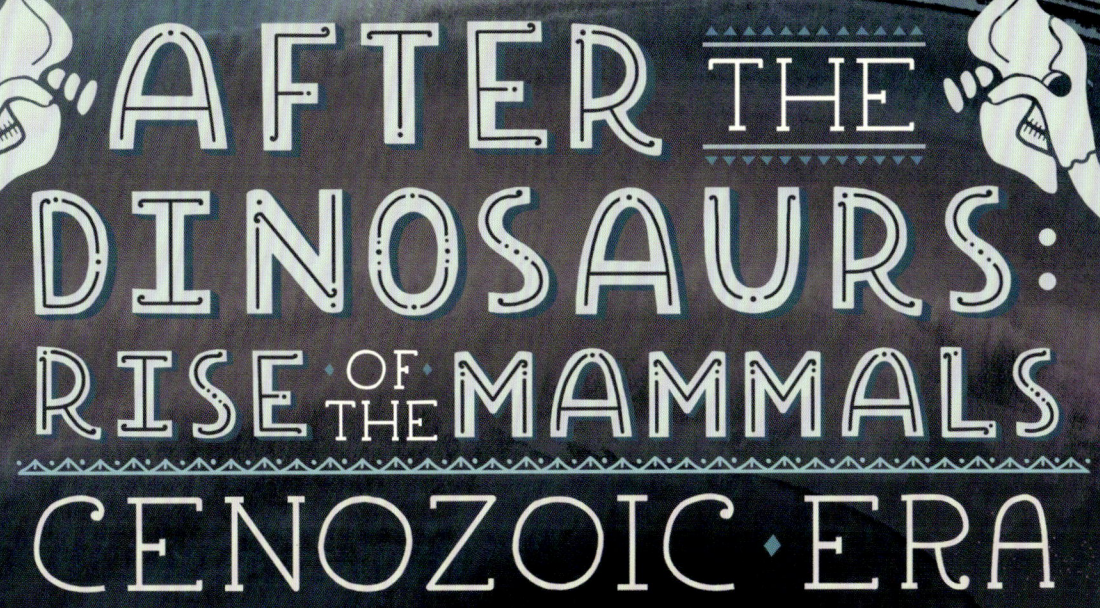

AFTER THE DINOSAURS: RISE OF THE MAMMALS

CENOZOIC · ERA

66 MILLION YEARS AGO TO TODAY

A woolly mammoth has been separated from the herd. In the brush, the hungry eyes of predators watch her, waiting to pounce. But it's not the expected saber-toothed cats lying in wait, but instead an even more fearsome predator: humans. A small group of *Homo sapiens* lunge at the hairy beast with spears. This prehistoric ice age scene could have happened more than 100,000 years ago, which is ancient history to us but just a blink of an eye in geological time. The Cenozoic Era is the chapter in Earth's history when mammals evolved in the absence of dinosaurs.

By the end of the dinosaurs' Mesozoic Era, the three main mammal groups were already established: the monotremes (mammals that lay eggs), marsupials (mammals that incubate and carry their young in a pouch), and placentals (mammals that give live birth from their womb). But these milk-making, furry, warm-blooded creatures were evolutionarily stuck. The largest true mammal from the Mesozoic was only the size of a badger. The asteroid impact would change everything. Mass extinction of large dinosaurs gave the mammal group a fighting chance. Without all those hungry reptiles to hide from, mammals found themselves in an empty playing field, rapidly evolving. As a result, an abundance of new species emerged quickly.

During the Cenozoic Era, the planet transformed into our modern icehouse Earth with large polar ice caps. Mammals evolved to conquer every ecological niche available. About 300,000 years ago, a group of primates evolved into highly intelligent, modern humans. Through collective learning, passed down from generations, humanity has created art, studied the universe, and transformed the world like no other species.

········· GEOLOGICAL TIME SCALE ·········

538.8 MYA

NOW

66 MYA

23 MYA

2.58 MYA

PHANEROZOIC EON

CENOZOIC ERA

PALEÓGENE PERIOD

QUATERNARY PERIOD

NEOGENE PERIOD

MESONYX→

VINTATHERIUM

NOTHARCTUS→

CYRILAVIS

SMILODECTES→

THE PALEOGENE PERIOD

PALAEOCHIROPTERYX

66 MILLION YEARS TO 23 MILLION YEARS AGO

After the dust settled from the environmental doom caused by the asteroid impact, the dinosaurs' reign was over. From the ashes small rat-looking mammal survivors would come out of their burrows. With little competition, mammals diversified and spread globally.

By the Middle Paleogene, mammals had adapted to live on land, fly in the air, and inhabit the ocean. Around 47 mya, *Ambulocetus*, nicknamed the "the walking whale," paddled out to sea. In the tropical forests of North America, early primates, like *Northarctus*, swung from tree branches as the earliest bats darted above. In the dense forests, mammals grew large, like the plant-eating megafauna *Uintatherium*, which grew to the size of a modern rhino. And the wolf-like carnivore, *Mesonyx*, prowled open woodland.

The Paleogene was a time of mountains rising and climate fluctuations. As tectonic plates collided, the Rocky Mountains and the Himalayan range towered skyward. The polar ice caps began to form 33 mya, and Earth started to significantly cool down. For the first time in Earth's history, an abundance of grasslands blanketed the globe. The ancestors of cats, dogs, elephants, and other mammals roamed these new savannahs. The hot greenhouse period was over, and the world entered its current icehouse state. The world was cooling down.

OROHIPPUS

BOREALOSUCHUS

THE PALEOGENE PERIOD
LAND AND SEA

While the Early Paleogene was hotter than today and supported expansive rainforests, toward the end of the period the global climate significantly cooled. Brand-new grasslands replaced forests on a grand scale. Although grasses existed during the Cretaceous Period in small patches, the Paleogene saw the first large-scale meadows and fields. Grass is a difficult food to digest, and many species could not handle the transition. A group of hooved mammals called ruminants would evolve a special chamber in their stomach that allowed them to digest tough plants and chew their cud (just like a modern cow). Meanwhile, predators that could sprint and run long distances on the open plains would rule the hunt. In the fields of North America 26 mya, *Hyaenodon* would rush unsuspecting grazers like primitive camels and the three-toed horse *Miohippus*. This was just the beginning for a new world covered in grass.

WAS 1 TO 2 FT. TALL

THE EARLIEST-KNOWN HORSE WAS *EOHIPPUS* (55 MYA TO 45 MYA), WHOSE NAME MEANS "THE DAWN HORSE."

FUN FACTS:

One of the largest land mammals that ever lived was *Paraceratherium* (34 mya to 23 mya). It was five times bigger than the average elephant.

PERSON FOR SCALE

17 FT. TALL AND 16 TONS

6 FT. TALL

MAY HAVE USED BEAK TO CRACK HARD SEEDS AND NUTS.

Birds of the Cenozoic evolved from the avian dinosaur survivors, including *Gastornis* (55 mya to 50 mya), a giant flightless bird.

Around 55 mya, global temperatures skyrocketed by 9°F, likely caused by a sudden release of methane gas from undersea volcanoes. Lasting about 100,000 years, this period was the hottest the Cenozoic Era had ever been.

CALLED THE PALEOCENE-EOCENE THERMAL MAXIMUM

SCIENTISTS STUDY IT TO SEE HOW CURRENT GLOBAL WARMING COULD CHANGE MODERN ECOSYSTEMS.

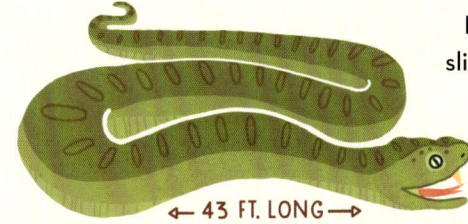

From 60 mya to 58 mya slithered the longest snake ever, the *Titanoboa*.

43 FT. LONG

RUN

STORIES OF DISCOVERY:

ROUND FINGERTIPS WITH NAILS AND OPPOSABLE THUMBS

BIG EYE SOCKETS FOR NOCTURNAL SIGHT

DARWINIUS

FOSSIL INFORMALLY NAMED IDA AFTER DR. HURUM'S DAUGHTER, WHO ALSO HAD HER BABY TEETH

Forty-seven million years ago, a small primate now called *Darwinius* was perched in a tree while eating a juicy fruit. Today this *Darwinius* is better known by the nickname Ida and is the most complete primate fossil to ever be discovered. Even Ida's last meal was fossilized in her stomach! The fossil was found in 1983 in the Messel Pit of Germany. In 2007, Dr. Jørn Hurum convinced the Natural History Museum in Oslo, Norway, to purchase the fossil for examination. Ida's remains are significant to understanding primate evolution. The fossil dates to the time when primates split into two main subgroups: Strepsirrhini (wet-nosed primates like lemurs and bush babies) and Haplorhini (dry-nosed primates like monkeys, apes, and humans). Ida showed features of both. Some scientists think she is a transitional missing link fossil, while others think she is a primitive lemur.

THE PALEOGENE PERIOD
CREATURE FEATURE

IT ONLY LOOKS LIKE A RHINO, BUT IS IN FACT MORE CLOSELY RELATED TO ELEPHANTS AND MANATEES.

ARSINOITHERIUM
PLACENTAL MAMMAL
35 MYA TO 27 MYA
11 ½ FT. LONG

PHIOMIA
PLACENTAL MAMMAL
37 MYA TO 30 MYA
16 FT. LONG

IT'S A PRIMITIVE ELEPHANT!

MOERITHERIUM
PLACENTAL MAMMAL
41 MYA TO 34 MYA
10 FT. LONG

IT LOOKS LIKE A HEAVY TAPIR, BUT IT'S A PRIMITIVE ELEPHANT!

AFROTHERIA:

Africa was an island continent during the Paleogene, and the group of mammals that evolved in isolation there are members of the superorder Afrotheria. This includes animals like primitive elephants, sea cows, golden moles, and more!

SEA COW

GOLDEN MOLE

AFRICA

THE EVOLUTION OF WHALES

THE SCIENTIFIC TERM FOR THE WHALE INFRAORDER IS CETACEA.

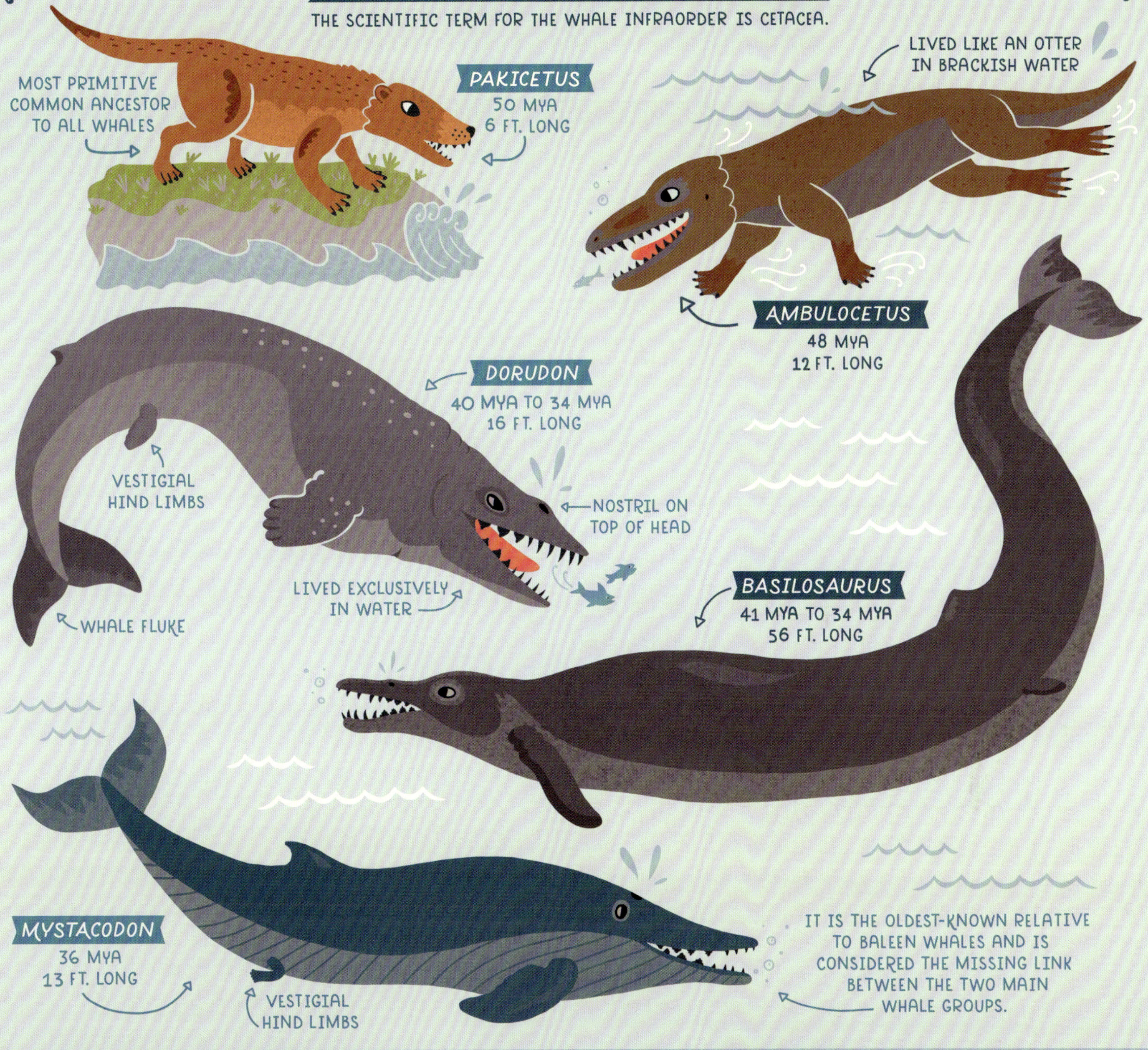

MOST PRIMITIVE COMMON ANCESTOR TO ALL WHALES

PAKICETUS
50 MYA
6 FT. LONG

LIVED LIKE AN OTTER IN BRACKISH WATER

AMBULOCETUS
48 MYA
12 FT. LONG

DORUDON
40 MYA TO 34 MYA
16 FT. LONG

VESTIGIAL HIND LIMBS

NOSTRIL ON TOP OF HEAD

LIVED EXCLUSIVELY IN WATER

WHALE FLUKE

BASILOSAURUS
41 MYA TO 34 MYA
56 FT. LONG

MYSTACODON
36 MYA
13 FT. LONG

VESTIGIAL HIND LIMBS

IT IS THE OLDEST-KNOWN RELATIVE TO BALEEN WHALES AND IS CONSIDERED THE MISSING LINK BETWEEN THE TWO MAIN WHALE GROUPS.

FROM LAND TO WATER!

The largest animal in the history of Earth is the blue whale, which swims our oceans today! In the weightlessness of the ocean, mammals would eventually beat the dinosaurs in size. This evolutionary transition from land back into the water happened during the Paleogene Period.

Fifty million years ago, a wolf-like land mammal called *Pakicetus* would become the common ancestor of all whales. It likely hunted for fishes along shallow coasts. Over millions of years, its offspring also hunted in the water and passed on genes that favored aquatic traits. Legs for walking slowly morphed into flippers for swimming. Nostrils moved higher up and further back to form blow holes. In only 10 million years,

BLUE WHALE
1.5 MYA TO TODAY
110 FT. LONG

WEIGHS UP TO 200 TONS

animals related to *Pakicetus* had evolved to exclusively live in the sea, like the ancient whale *Dorudon* (40 mya).

About 34 mya, whales split into two major groups: the toothed whales and the baleen whales. Toothed whales would evolve into today's dolphins, orcas, porpoises, sperm whales, and beaked whales. Baleen whales had hair-like bristles instead of teeth, perfect for filter feeding on plankton and krill. This baleen lineage includes the biggest animals, like the modern blue whale.

THE NEOGENE PERIOD

23 MILLION YEARS TO 2.58 MILLION YEARS AGO

APATOSAGITTARIUS

Grasslands emerged as a new kind of terrain during the Cenozoic Era. The climate became colder and drier, killing off the vast rainforests. These arid conditions favored hardy grass plants that required less water than dense forests. Prairies and savannahs spread across millions of square miles and forced mammals to adapt to a new ecosystem. Grazing animals evolved to take advantage of this grassy food that grew back from its root system no matter how many times it was mowed down. The open plains made long-distance running necessary for survival. Horses like *Merychippus* had powerfully fast legs. Herds of animals found safety in numbers from pouncing predators like the vicious bear-dog, *Amphicyon*. In Africa, shrinking jungles and growing savannahs gave our own primate ancestors, the early hominids, the evolutionary push to walk upright on two legs.

Toward the end of the Neogene Period, tectonic activity revealed a thin stretch of land called the Panama Land Bridge, which connects North and South America. For the first time, animals and plants could move back and forth between these continents in a massive migration called the Great American Biotic Interchange. While polar snowstorms locked away water in glaciers and ice caps, the Panama Land Bridge also physically separated the warm waters of the Atlantic Ocean from the cool waters of the Pacific Ocean. This changed ocean currents and weather patterns, which many scientists believe further contributed to global cooling and oncoming ice ages.

HORNED GOPHER

THE NEOGENE PERIOD
LAND AND SEA

As grasslands spread, the cool climate of the Neogene transformed the forests. Across North America and Eurasia, seasonal trees like maples and oaks filled temperate forests, which looked as colorful and familiar as today's fall foliage. In the ocean a new type of large brown algae called kelp grew. Kelp forests filled the shallow coastal waters, and this new habitat was home to sea otters and sea cows.

BROWN ALGAE

ENHYDRA

During the Neogene, all modern primate lineages of apes and monkeys diverged. Around 7 mya, hominids, the group humans belong to, split off from chimpanzees. While the ancestors of modern chimps continued to swing from trees in the jungles, hominids like *Australopithecus* adapted to the savannah grasslands by walking upright. Walking on two legs is energy efficient and makes walking long distances easier. It also frees up the hands to make and hold tools.

FUN FACTS:

The bizarre-looking *Chalicotherium* (13 mya to 5.3 mya) belongs to the only group of animals known to evolve claws from a hooved animal.

WALKED HUNCHED OVER LIKE AN APE

ARDIPITHECUS 4.5 MYA TO 4.3 MYA

Many early hominid remains have been discovered, but little is known about how they lived. Scientists hypothesize that these basal hominids were partly bipedal.

Otodus megalodon (23 mya to 3.6 mya) was the largest shark to ever live on Earth. Its mouth was filled with 276 teeth, and everything was on the menu.

50 FT LONG

OH NO

STORIES OF DISCOVERY:

CAST OF THE LAETOLI FOOTPRINTS

LUCY

BASED ON HER HIP BONES AND TEETH, WE KNOW THAT LUCY WAS A FEMALE IN EARLY ADULTHOOD.

MARY LEAKEY

3½ FT. TALL

AUSTRALOPITHECUS AFARENSIS

IN 1978, FOOTPRINTS OF *AUSTRALOPITHECUS AFARENSIS* WERE FOUND BY PALEOLOGIST MARY LEAKEY, CONFIRMING THAT EARLY HOMINIDS WALKED UPRIGHT.

In 1974, "Lucy in the Sky with Diamonds" by the Beatles rang out from an Ethiopian campsite in celebration of one of the most significant fossils finds in human evolution! The team led by paleoanthropologist Donald Johanson had just spent weeks unearthing the bones of an early hominid from 3.18 mya. It was 40 percent of a complete female *Australopithecus afarensis* skeleton—the most intact primitive hominid fossil ever found. The team informally named the fossil Lucy, inspired by the song, and she quickly became famous!

Scientists have reconstructed Lucy's entire skeleton using bone fragments. Since then, several more fossils belonging to *A. afarensis* have been found to help complete the picture. The species lived from 3.85 mya to 2.95 mya. Although *Australopithecus* is not the earliest member of the hominid family, we know for certain that they primarily walked on two feet, while earlier species may have only done so part-time. By studying Lucy, paleontologists determined that hominids evolved the ability to walk upright long before early humans developed big brains and intellect.

THYLACOSMILUS
MARSUPIAL MAMMAL
5.3 MYA TO 2.6 MYA
4 FT. LONG

SABER TEETH GREW
CONSTANTLY
DURING ITS LIFE.

A SCAVENGER
IN THE
GRASSLANDS
OF SOUTH
AMERICA

ALSO KNOWN AS
A TASMANIAN TIGER

THYLACINUS
MARSUPIAL MAMMAL
4 MYA TO 20TH CENTURY
4¼ FT. LONG

THE LAST
THYLACINUS
DIED IN 1936
AT A ZOO.

LIVED IN THE EUCALYPTUS
FORESTS IN AUSTRALIA

RELATED TO
WOMBATS
AND KOALAS

EURYZYGOMA DUNENSE
MARSUPIAL MAMMAL
5 MYA TO 1.5 MYA
8 FT. LONG

NIMBADON
MARSUPIAL MAMMAL
15 MYA TO 12 MYA
3 FT. LONG

MARSUPIAL MADNESS

During the Neogene Period, tons of marsupials lived on the island continents of Australia and South America! Placental mammals incubate offspring in their womb and give birth to live, fully developed babies. In contrast, marsupials' young are born undeveloped and then climb into their mother's pouch to nurse and grow. Placental mammals have a huge advantage over marsupials, and placentals make up the overwhelming majority of mammal species living today. During the Neogene, marsupials evolved and thrived in isolated conditions, often resembling their placental counterparts. Saber-toothed marsupials like *Thylacosmilus* prowled South America and resembled the more famous saber-toothed cats like *Smilodon*. Although they do not share a significant common ancestor, similar evolutionary pressures gave these carnivores nearly the same body plan. Australia is still home to the largest living marsupial population on the planet.

AGILE WALLABY
4 MYA TO TODAY
2¾ FT. LONG

MARSUPIALS'
YOUNG NURSE
IN POUCH

PLATYBELODON

PLACENTAL MAMMAL
16 MYA TO 11 MYA

←-- 20 FT. LONG --→

FED ON SOFT
SWAMP PLANTS IN
AFRICA AND ASIA.

FLAT SHOVEL-
LIKE TUSK

STRANGE ELEPHANTS

The order of animals that includes the elephant family goes back
60 million years. During the Neogene Period, primitive elephants and
their elephant-like cousins roamed the savannah, shoveling grass
into their mouths with their long trunks. They would have looked like
a funhouse-mirror version of today's elephants—some had too many
tusks, while others had tusks that were so highly specialized they
looked almost silly. Today's Asian and African elephants are some
of the last remaining megafauna on the planet.

PLATYBELODON
SKULL

OTHER PRIMITIVE ELEPHANT RELATIVES

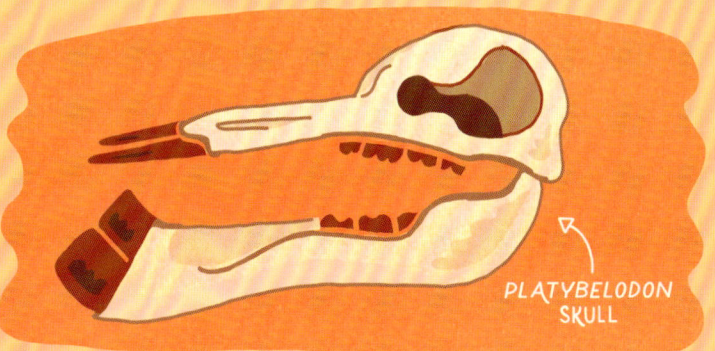

DEINOTHERIUM

PLACENTAL MAMMAL
14 MYA TO 1 MYA
14 FT. TALL

TUSK GREW FROM
LOWER JAW.
SHORTER TRUNK

GOMPHOTHERIUM

PLACENTAL MAMMAL
18 MYA TO 4 MYA
9½ FT. TALL

ITS 4 TUSKS WERE
PROBABLY USED TO
STRIP PLANTS.

THE QUATERNARY PERIOD

2.58 MILLION YEARS AGO TO TODAY

Brrrrr! Welcome to the ice ages of the Quaternary Period, when ice sheets covered North America, Europe, and Asia. Megafauna from this period looked as though they had come out of a fantasy novel, having adapted to cold weather by becoming large and furry. There were Irish elk whose antlers spanned 12 feet wide, as well as large saber-toothed cats with knife-like teeth, woolly rhinos, and mammoths. These animals lived alongside—and were even hunted by—our prehistoric human ancestors.

The Quaternary, our current period in geological time, is when modern humans evolved. Early humans did not have sharp teeth or claws, but instead relied on tools and teamwork to take down large animals. The ability to access protein-rich foods was necessary to fuel a larger brain. Tools continue to make humans one of the most adaptable animals on the planet.

Modern humans, also known as *Homo sapiens*, evolved in Africa 300,000 years ago, and migrated to every part of the globe. Around 10,000 years ago, nearly all the megafauna became extinct. Earth's climate was warming toward a period of interglaciation, when ice caps receded and cold-weather habitats shrunk. Meanwhile, prehistoric humans continued to migrate and often overhunted large prey to feed their growing populations. Both warm weather and encroaching humans spelled doom for the giant ice age animals.

What makes humanity unique is our ability to pass down and improve upon technology with every generation. Twelve thousand years ago, humans invented ways to cultivate crops and domesticate animals. Since then, people have continued to reshape the natural world to suit their needs. Today, all of Earth's ecosystems have been transformed by human activity.

SNOWY OWL

EUROPEAN MINK

HOMO SAPIENS

THE QUATERNARY PERIOD
LAND AND SEA

Technically, we are currently living in an ice age—even though it may not feel like it on a hot summer day. In the past 2.6 million years there have been five major ice ages. The last glacial maximum was 20,000 years ago, when 8 percent of Earth was covered in ice sheets. Periods of glaciation last about 100,000 years and are followed by interglaciation periods when ice retreats, which last about 20,000 years. Ice ages are caused by many factors: the tilt of Earth's axis, ocean currents, and the amount of sunlight reflected off white sea ice. The balance of carbon dioxide and oxygen in the atmosphere also has an impact on the global climate.

With each freeze-thaw cycle during the Quaternary Period, the wilderness was transformed. Animals had to adapt to a changing landscape, migrate, or perish. Around 11,700 years ago, Earth entered our current interglaciation period, with warmer weather and smaller ice caps. For large hairy animals like the mastodon, this would be fatal.

In recent centuries of the Quaternary Period, human activity has impacted the global climate. In the 1700s, the Industrial Revolution spurred the burning of fossil fuels to power new factories, ships, and trains. Burning fossil fuels releases warming greenhouse gasses like carbon dioxide and methane into the atmosphere. Over hundreds of years, this continued industrial activity has contributed to the ice caps shrinking at for wildlife to adapt.

FUN FACTS:

As ice age glaciers melted, they created lakes and carved landscapes and eerily flat plains. As glaciers move and melt, they leave behind out-of-place gigantic rocks in a landscape called glacial erratics.

HOW DID THAT ROCK GET HERE?

← MEGATHERIUM LIVED 35 MYA TO 11,000 YEARS AGO.

The gigantic ground sloths are an iconic ice age animal. The largest, *Megatherium* of South America, was 20 feet long and ate leaves and grasses.

While most mammoths had already gone extinct around 10,000 years ago, the pygmy mammoth lived isolated on the Channel Islands in California until 3,000 years ago.

IT DESCENDED FROM THE MAINLAND COLUMBIAN MAMMOTH, BUT EVOLVED TO BE SMALL ON ISOLATED ISLANDS.

COLUMBIAN MAMMOTH 14 FT. TALL

PYGMY MAMMOTH 4 ½ TO 7 FT. TALL

STORIES OF DISCOVERY:

In 2022, when gold miners dug into the hard permafrost of northwestern Canada, they never expected to find something even more valuable than precious metal—a perfectly preserved baby mammoth from 30,000 years ago! By studying the permafrost (the frozen soil) where this 1-month-old female mammoth was found, geologists hypothesize that she likely strayed from the herd and became stuck in a mud pit. When the mud froze over, her remains became an ice mummy. Unlike a fossil in rock, permafrost kept delicate soft tissue like skin, hair, and muscles intact. DNA can even be extracted from ice mummies and sequenced to better understand these animals.

The tiny mammoth's remains were found in the traditional territory of the Yukon First Nation, Tr'ondëk Hwëch'in, who have named her *Nun cho ga* (big baby animal). Together, the Tr'ondëk Hwëch'in leaders, the local government, geologists, and the miners have continued to cooperate to further study this area. They have uncovered frozen wolf pups from 57,000 years ago and other ice age animals like giant camels and caribou.

THE QUATERNARY PERIOD
CREATURE FEATURE

NICKNAMED THE HANDY MAN BECAUSE STONE TOOLS HAVE BEEN FOUND NEAR THE FOSSILS

OLDOWAN TOOLS

LIVED ALONGSIDE *HOMO ERECTUS*, AND IT IS DEBATED WHETHER OR NOT THEY ARE DIRECT ANCESTORS TO MODERN HUMANS.

HOMO HABILIS

2.4 MYA TO 1.4 MYA
3 ⅓ TO 4 ½ FT. TALL
FOUND IN AFRICA

EARLIEST KNOWN HUMANS TO HAVE MODERN BODY PROPORTIONS

ACHEULEAN STONE TOOLS

HAND AXES

HOMO ERECTUS

1.89 MILLION TO 110,000 YEARS AGO
UP TO 6 FT. TALL
FOUND IN AFRICA AND ASIA

EARLIEST EVIDENCE OF CAMPFIRES. THEY ARE USED TO COOK, FOR WARMTH, AS MEETING PLACES FOR SOCIAL GATHERINGS, AND FOR DEFENSE FROM HOSTILE ANIMALS.

TERRA AMATA SHELTER
400,000 YEARS OLD, FRANCE

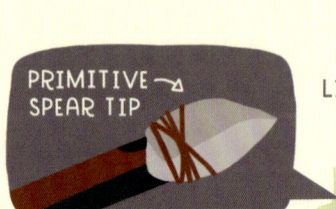

PRIMITIVE SPEAR TIP

HUNTED ANIMALS MUCH LARGER THAN THEMSELVES, LIKE ELEPHANTS AND RHINOS.

HOMO HEIDELBERGENSIS

700,000 TO 200,000 YEARS AGO
UP TO 6 FT. TALL
FOUND IN EUROPE, AFRICA, AND POSSIBLY EAST ASIA

ONE OF THE EARLIEST-KNOWN BUILT SHELTERS

PREHISTORIC HUMANS:

The evolution from the earliest hominids to modern humans is not a straight line. The human evolutionary tree is a messy one, with many branches that often intertwine. Thousands of primitive and early human fossils have been studied to better understand our own origins. *Homo habilis, Homo erectus,* and *Homo heidelbergensis* are just a few of the notable prehistoric species.

HOMO SAPIENS

THE WORD FOR THE GENUS "*HOMO*" MEANS "HUMAN" IN LATIN.

HOMO NEANDERTHALENSIS

400,000 TO 40,000 YEARS AGO
UP TO 5½ FT. TALL
FOUND IN EUROPE AND ASIA

MADE JEWELRY AND
SOPHISTICATED TOOLS
FOR HUNTING

COLD-WEATHER
ADAPTATIONS INCLUDED
LARGE NOSE CAVITIES TO
WARM AIR BEFORE IT
REACHED THE LUNGS AND
SHORTER, STOCKIER BODIES
THAN *HOMO SAPIENS*.

MODERN HUMANS: *HOMO SAPIENS*

300,000 YEARS AGO TO TODAY
FIRST EMERGED IN AFRICA AND
THEN MIGRATED WORLDWIDE

STONE-TIPPED
ARROW
64,000
YEARS AGO
SOUTH AFRICA

MADE SPECIALIZED REFINED STONE
TOOLS LIKE FISH HOOKS, SEWING
NEEDLES, AND BOWS AND ARROWS

THE OLDEST-KNOWN CAVE ART, "DRAWING
OF A PIG AND TWO PEOPLE" IS FROM
51,200 YEARS AGO IN INDONESIA.

HUMANS BEGAN CULTIVATING
CROPS AND DOMESTICATING
ANIMALS 12,000 YEARS AGO.

COEXISTING PREHISTORIC HUMANS

Neanderthals are just one of the prehistoric human species that lived alongside modern humans (*Homo sapiens*). The Denisovans (195,000 years ago) are another intelligent human species that lived in Asia. Although very few Denisovan fossils have been found, DNA analysis has taught us a lot. Neanderthals and Denisovans had children with *Homo sapiens*, so they are distant relatives of modern humans. All traces of Neanderthals and Denisovans disappeared around 40,000 years ago. Although the exact reason is still a mystery, most likely they were outcompeted by *Homo sapiens*. Today, very small traces of their DNA live on. Some people from Europe and Asia have up to 4 percent of Neanderthal DNA, while some people from East Asia and Oceania have up to 5.6 percent of Denisovan DNA. Every single person on Earth today is descended from early *Homo sapiens*, the modern humans who first evolved in Africa.

THE HOLOCENE EPOCH

The Holocene Epoch is the last 11,700 years of Earth history. It started when the natural warming of the climate caused an interglacial period. This epoch has been defined by humanity gaining new technology to form civilizations.

HUMAN IMPACT AND THE SIXTH MASS EXTINCTION

Twelve thousand years ago, modern humans began farming and domesticating livestock. Surpluses and control over food meant a boom in population and more time to spend on inventing tools, creating art, and more! From farms, towns formed, which turned into cities and empires. With each generation, technology has improved to help transform the natural world even more efficiently for human comfort.

Throughout Earth's history there have been five mass extinction events. Many scientists believe we are currently in or approaching a sixth mass extinction event caused by the impact of human actions like pollution, destruction of habitat, and overhunting. In addition, the burning of fossil fuels contributes to a rapidly warming climate. Scientists estimate that right now the extinction rate is between 100 and 1,000 times higher than the natural baseline. Here are several ways humans have negatively affected biodiversity.

OVERHUNTING

As modern humans spread around the globe, they often overhunted large prey and outcompeted other species for resources. Many scientists attribute the combination of a naturally warming interglacial climate and human activity for the extinction of nearly all ice age megafauna. Poaching and overfishing continue to be big problems today.

R.I.P.
PASSENGER PIGEON

R.I.P.
CALIFORNIA GRIZZLY BEAR

R.I.P.
STELLER'S SEA COW

EXTINCT FROM OVERHUNTING

LOSS OF WILD SPACES

The overexploitation of natural resources through deforestation, encroaching cities, and suburban sprawl has forced wildlife to migrate away from their shrinking natural habits.

LARGE-SCALE FARMING

For thousands of years, humans have bred animals as livestock and transformed wild habitats into farmland. This turns biodiverse areas into landscapes with only a few species of animals and plants.

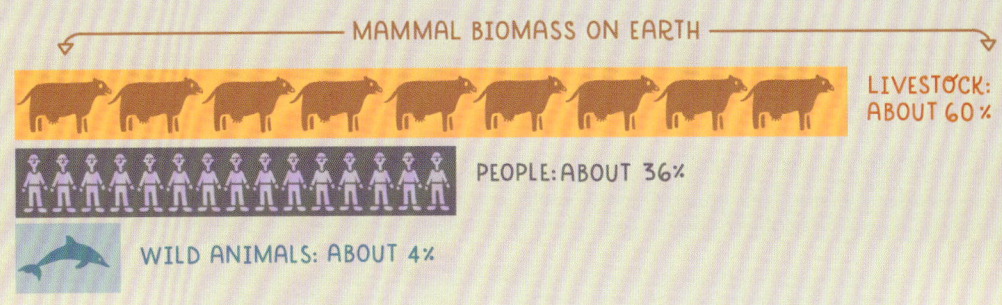

MAMMAL BIOMASS ON EARTH

LIVESTOCK: ABOUT 60%

PEOPLE: ABOUT 36%

WILD ANIMALS: ABOUT 4%

CLIMATE CHANGE

Since the Industrial Revolution, people have been burning fossil fuels for energy. These fuels are made from dead plants and animals that absorbed carbon hundreds of millions of years ago. When these fuels are burned, it releases ancient, long-stored greenhouse gasses into our modern atmosphere. Throughout Earth's history, the shift in the balance of oxygen versus carbon dioxide has created extinction events. Today, our planet is getting hotter at a quicker pace than that of natural interglaciation and is warming ten times faster than it has since the age of the dinosaurs. Such rapid change makes it difficult for scientists to accurately predict climate changes. What we do know is that humanity evolved on an icehouse Earth that has polar ice caps. As we use our natural resources, we need to also preserve the ecosystems that have allowed people to thrive in the first place.

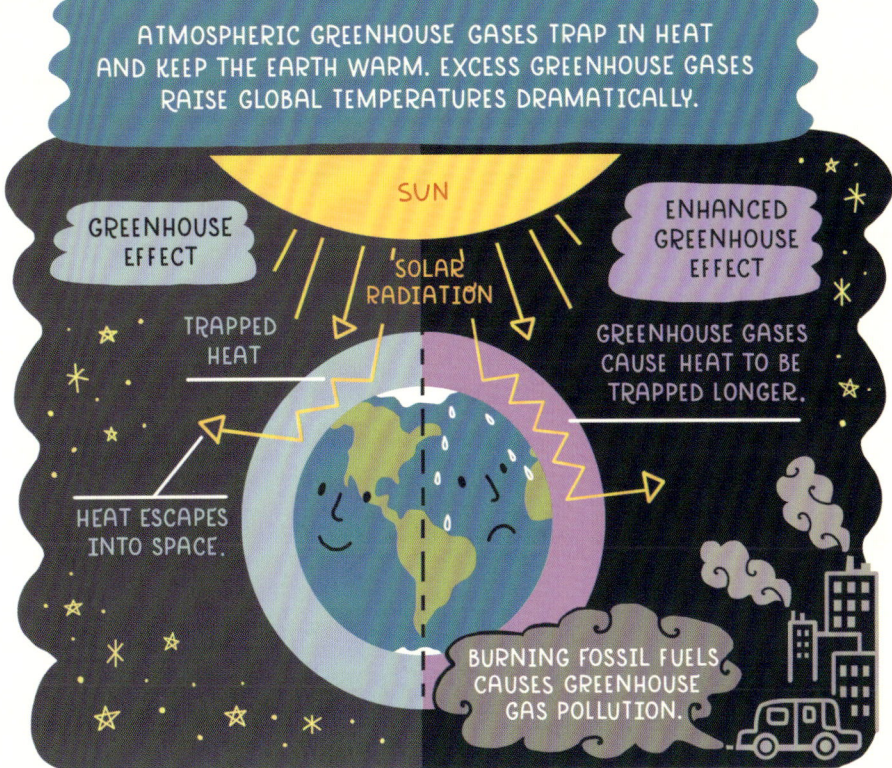

ATMOSPHERIC GREENHOUSE GASES TRAP IN HEAT AND KEEP THE EARTH WARM. EXCESS GREENHOUSE GASES RAISE GLOBAL TEMPERATURES DRAMATICALLY.

SUN

GREENHOUSE EFFECT

ENHANCED GREENHOUSE EFFECT

SOLAR RADIATION

TRAPPED HEAT

GREENHOUSE GASES CAUSE HEAT TO BE TRAPPED LONGER.

HEAT ESCAPES INTO SPACE.

BURNING FOSSIL FUELS CAUSES GREENHOUSE GAS POLLUTION.

PROTECTING OUR PLANET

Humanity is one of the most adaptable species in Earth's history! Let's use our big brains, technology, and teamwork to protect our planet.

LEARN MORE ABOUT OUR PLANET! FUND RESEARCH AND SCIENCE!

NATIONAL PARK

PROTECT WILD SPACES!

ALTERNATIVE ENERGY

SOLAR

WIND

HYDRO

NUCLEAR

CIRCULAR ECONOMY: REUSE, REPAIR, AND RECYCLE!

KEEP EXPLORING

Learning about deep time is a reminder of how precious our current moment on Earth is. Many worlds existed here on Earth long before we arrived. There are many more mysteries beneath the rocks. What is currently known about deep time is small compared to what is still left to uncover. On average, paleontologists discover a brand-new dinosaur every two weeks. By learning about our long-buried past, we can better understand our own place on this planet and in the universe.

SOURCES AND RESOURCES

Want to learn more? Here are some places that I visited for inspiration and sources I used to research this book. This is just a start to further pique your interest! For worksheets, coloring pages, and even more resources, check out my website: rachelignotofskydesign.com

ADVENTURES AND MUSEUMS:

Arches National Park
5 miles north of Moab on US 191,
Moab, UT 84532

Cleveland-Lloyd Dinosaur Quarry
125 S 600 W, Price, UT 84501

Dinosaur National Monument
11625 E 1500 S, Jensen, UT 84035

U-Dig Fossils Quarry
Death Canyon Road, Delta, UT 84624

Field Museum
1400 S Dusable Lake Shore Drive, Chicago, IL 60605
fieldmuseum.org

La Brea Tar Pits and Museum
5801 Wilshire Boulevard, Los Angeles, CA 90036
tarpits.org

Natural History Museum of Los Angeles County
900 Exposition Boulevard, Los Angeles, CA 90007
nhm.org

San Diego Natural History Museum
1788 El Prado, Balboa Park, San Diego, CA 92101
sdnhm.org

Smithsonian National Museum of Natural History
10th St. & Constitution Ave. NW, Washington, DC 20560
si.edu

BOOKS:

Brusatte, Stephen. *The Rise and Fall of the Dinosaurs: A New History of Their Lost World*. New York: William Morrow, 2018.

Brusatte, Stephen. *The Rise and Reign of the Mammals: A New History, from the Shadow of the Dinosaurs to Us*. Boston: Mariner Books, 2022.

Dinosaurs and Prehistoric Life: The Definitive Visual Guide to Prehistoric Animals. New York: DK Publishing, 2023.

Fortey, Richard. *Trilobite! Eyewitness to Evolution*. New York: Alfred Knopf, 2000.

Knoll, Andrew H. *A Brief History of Earth: Four Billion Years in Eight Chapters*. New York: Custom House, 2021.

McGhee, George R. *When the Invasion of Land Failed: The Legacy of the Devonian Extinctions*. New York: Columbia University Press, 2013.

Pellant, Chris. *Rocks & Minerals*. New York: DK Publishing, 2021.

Pim, Keiron. *Dinosaurs—the Grand Tour: Everything Worth Knowing about Dinosaurs from Aardonyx to Zuniceratops*, 2nd ed. New York: The Experiment, 2019.

Randall, David K. *The Monster's Bones: The Discovery of T. rex and How It Shook Our World*. New York: W. W. Norton & Company, 2022.

Walker, Cyril, and David Ward. *Fossils*. New York: DK Publishing, 2002.

ACKNOWLEDGMENTS:

First, I would like to thank my husband and business partner, Thomas Mason, for his help with this project. Not only was he my research assistant, but he organized countless trips to museums and dig sites. His edits, suggestions, and late nights with rewrites and coffee made this project possible!

THOMAS MASON →

A huge thank-you to paleontologist Thomas R. Holtz. He was the fact-checker on this project, and his expertise on dinosaurs and geological time made this book amazing!

Thank you to my editor, Kaitlin Ketchum, and the rest of the Ten Speed publishing team for all their help putting this book out into the world. There is so much work that goes on behind the scenes making a book a reality! And a big thank-you to my literary agent, Monica Odom.

ABOUT THE AUTHOR

Rachel Ignotofsky is a *New York Times* best-selling author and illustrator who makes work about science and history.

FOR MORE VISIT RachelIgnotofskyDesign.com

MORE BOOKS BY RACHEL IGNOTOFSKY

WOMEN IN SCIENCE

WOMEN IN SPORTS

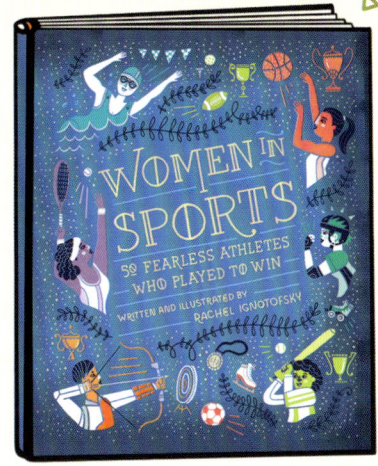

WOMEN IN ART

WHAT'S INSIDE A FLOWER?

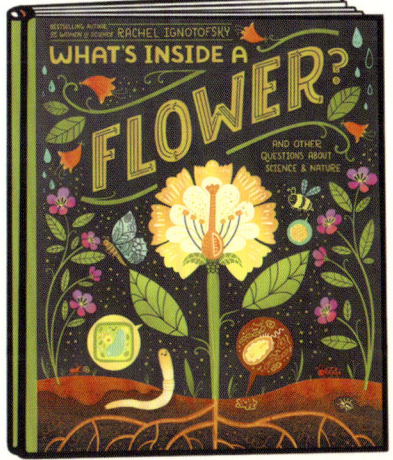

WHAT'S INSIDE A CATERPILLAR COCOON?

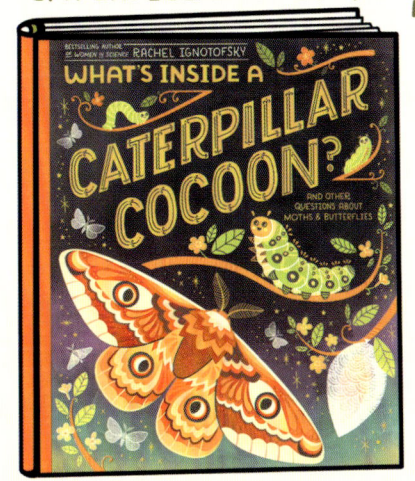

WHAT'S INSIDE A BIRD'S NEST?

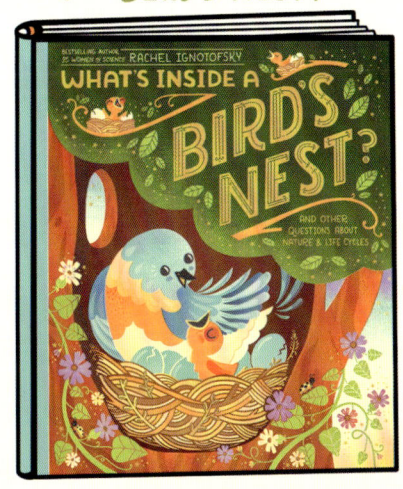

THE WONDROUS WORKINGS OF PLANET EARTH

THE HISTORY OF THE COMPUTER

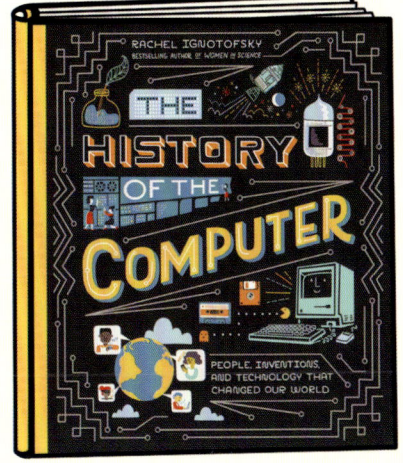

SCIENCE AND NATURE COLORING BOOKS

INDEX

Ten Speed Press
An imprint of the Crown Publishing Group
A division of Penguin Random House LLC
1745 Broadway
New York, NY 10019
tenspeed.com
penguinrandomhouse.com

Ten Speed Press and the Ten Speed Press colophon are registered trademarks of Penguin Random House LLC.

Typefaces: Rachel Ignotofsky's Rachel and House Industries' Neutraface Text

Library of Congress Control Number: 2025933652

Hardcover ISBN 978-1-9848-6175-7
eBook ISBN 978-1-9848-6176-4

Printed in China

Acquiring editor: Kaitlin Ketchum | Production editor: Serena Wang
Editorial assistant: Kausaur Fahimuddin
Designer: Francesca Truman | Production designer: Mari Gill | Art director: Chloe Rawlins
Production manager: Jane Chinn
Copyeditor: Lisa Brousseau | Proofreaders: Mikayla Butchart, Katy Miller,
and Christina Caruccio
Indexer: Jay Kreider
Publicist: Felix Cruz | Marketer: Allison Renzulli

10 9 8 7 6 5 4 3 2 1

First Edition

The authorized representative in the EU for product safety and compliance is Penguin Random House Ireland, Morrison Chambers, 32 Nassau Street, Dublin D02 YH68, Ireland, https://eu-contact.penguin.ie.